WALES : A CELEBRATION

Wales : A Celebration

An anthology of poetry and prose

edited by
Dewi Roberts
with a foreword by
Jan Morris

Text: Authors/Anthology: Dewi Roberts

ISBN: 0-86381-608-8

Cover design: Sian Parri
Cover illustration: Aneurin Jones

First published in this format in 2000 by
Gwasg Carreg Gwalch, 12 Iard yr Orsaf, Llanrwst, Wales LL26 0EH
☎ 01492 642031   📠 01492 641502
✆ books@carreg-gwalch.co.uk   Website: www.carreg-gwalch.co.uk

For Sally and the staff of Tŷ Newydd

Foreword

Compiling an anthology about an entire nation must be rather like making a précis of some great work of literature – such an immense narrative to explain, such grand passages to represent, such a wealth of characters to introduce and nuances to reflect! Wales is surely as difficult a country as any to truncate in this way. It is small but it is very old, its history has been vivid with remarkable men and women, and its subtleties are endless. It is even harder, perhaps, to produce a Welsh anthology which is quite frankly introduced as a 'celebration', for ours is a country that has had more than its fair share of gush and fulsomeness, and actually much of the most entertaining writing about it has been decidedly unfriendly.

Dewi Roberts is an experienced and accomplished master of this deceptive genre, and now that he has tackled Wales as a whole he has avoided all the obvious pitfalls. Just a look at this book's roster of authors can assure us that, if we will find no deliciously maddening insults here, we will find no slushy sycophancy either. Authors from many Welsh centuries, from many backgrounds and from both of the national languages are represented here – poets from Dafydd ap Gwilym to Iwan Llwyd, novelists as varied as Caradoc Evans and Emyr Humphreys, historical writers as diverse as Gwyn Alf Williams and Shakespeare himself.

It is a celebration indeed, and as its author himself says, it is a declaration not just of fascination with the past of Wales, but of faith in its future.

Jan Morris

Introduction

Anthologists are probably among the most fortunate people working in the literary field. In the nature of things they do not experience the spasms of self-doubt and misgivings which afflict so many creative writers. This is my sixth venture into this genre and it is certainly one which has given me immense pleasure and satisfaction. Quite apart from anything else the process of selecting the material has greatly widened my reading about Wales, giving me fresh insights into many aspects of Welsh life and literature.

Here you will find poetry, prose fiction, historical accounts, autobiographical impressions, letters, diary extracts and journalism. The book covers a wide timespan, from bloody warfare in medieval North Wales to that historic rugby match in which Wales beat Argentina in the newly opened Millennium Stadium in Cardiff in 1999.

Readers will find both Welsh-language items in translation alongside both poetry and prose by Welsh writers in English.

Among the former are Dafydd ap Gwilym, John Ceiriog Hughes, Daniel Owen, Kate Roberts, Saunders Lewis, D.J. Williams, T.H. Parry-Williams, Waldo Williams, Gwenallt Jones, Islwyn Ffowc Ellis, and from a younger generation Menna Elfyn and Iwan Llwyd. Anglo-Welsh writers represented include Caradoc Evans, Gwyn Thomas, Glyn Jones, Leslie Norris, Gillian Clarke, R.S. Thomas, Jack Jones, Rhys Davies, Siân James and Emyr Humphreys.

Some English writers are also to be found here and certain of these have not previously appeared in anthologies produced in Wales. They include Macaulay, D.H. Lawrence, John Galsworthy, P.G. Wodehouse and John Wain.

In general terms this is a positive selection, as the title suggests. Even Macaulay, a true English Whig if ever there was one, is forced, despite previous misgivings, to admit some fondness for the Welsh people. Wodehouse, whose inimitable fiction is the quintessence of Englishness, writes of the Welsh voice 'penetrating a man's inner consciousness', a quote which should give all Welsh choirs new heart.

Not surprisingly the largest section is devoted to history and, as in all the other sections, I very much regretted having to leave so many items out for reasons of space. The fact that we have to understand our history and nationality in order to understand ourselves may seem like a pious platitude by now, but, none the less, it remains true. I have used an eclectic range of historical sources, including *The Mabinogion*, a vivid letter written by a knight in the service of Henry III, Shakespeare's portrayal of Glyndŵr, Marion Eames' account of the persecution of a witch, the Merthyr uprising described by Gwyn Alf Williams, as well as subsequent material focusing on events throughout Wales.

In devoting a section to culture, I think a word of explanation is needed, for nowadays the word can mean all things to all people. I use the word in a highly conventional way here, and it was almost inevitable that the language and language issues would form the basis for a number of the contributions. Few can have felt more passionately about the language than Saunders Lewis on whose powerful verse play *Buchedd Garmon* I have drawn. John Barnie makes a striking link between his knowledge of Welsh and his relationship with the landscape of Gwent; Dafydd Iwan writes of his singing career; John Wain describes a fictional character learning the language, while Grahame Davies writes of

'the genes of civilisation
defying death, determined to live'.

The sections on topography, people, and religion are self-explanatory. It is by deliberate choice that Dylan Thomas is excluded, for I feel that he has been over-exposed in other anthologies.

The future of the literary culture of Wales, in both languages, is vibrant as we enter another century and a new millennium. The literature of this small country deserves at least equal status to writing being produced in Scotland and Ireland. The Academi continues to promote the work of a worthy body of poets and novelists, the Tŷ Newydd writer's centre offers an invaluable service, while the publishing companies produce an increasing number of interesting, sometimes exceptional, new titles each year. Possibly in fifty years time a kindred spirit may compile a further celebratory anthology incorporating much of the work, which at this point in time, lies in a very promising future.

Dewi Roberts
Autumn 2000

Acknowledgements

Every attempt has been made to contact the owners of copyright in connection with the following items, but in certain cases this has not proved possible. We apologise for this and give our assurance that any omissions from this list will be rectified in any subsequent reprint.

Norman Nicholson's 'Wales' from *Five Rivers*, courtesy of Faber and Faber

Leslie Norris for an extract from 'Sing It Again, Wordsworth' from *The Girl from Cardigan* (Seren)

Jonah Jones for an extract from an essay from *Artists in Wales* edited by Meic Stephens (Gomer)

Ruth Bidgood for *Green Man at the Bwlch*

Mrs Gwen Watkins for *Ode to Swansea* by Vernon Watkins

Emyr Humphreys for two extracts from an essay included in *Artists in Wales* edited by Meic Stephens (Gomer); for 'Pastoral' included in *Collected Poems* (University of Wales Press) and for a passage from *Outside the House of Baal* (Seren)

The Estate of Wil Ifan for *The River and the Road* by Wil Ifan

The Estate of Amy Clampitt for *Mysterious Britain*

Richard Poole for 'Sheep in Blaenau Ffestiniog' from *Autobiographies and Explorations* (Headland) and 'Castell y Bere' from *Natural Histories* (Zenor)

Dannie Abse and Seren for *Return to Cardiff*

Christine Evans and Seren for *Llyn*

Peter Fraser and Dunlop Ltd and Random House UK Ltd for an extract from *The Cruise of the Nono* by Hilaire Belloc

Clyde Holmes for his previously unpublished poem *Guy Fawkes Night*

Nigel Jenkins for *Dafydd ap Gwilym Goes to Town*

Christopher Sinclair Stevenson for a passage from *Saint's Progress* by John Galsworthy

Laurence Pollinger for an extract from *St Mawr* by D.H. Lawrence

Mrs Myfanwy Lumsden for an extract from *The White Farm* by Geraint Goodwin

John Jones Publishing for an extract from *Feet in Chains* by Kate Roberts, translated by John Idris Jones and Idwal Walters

Jan Morris for extracts from *Wales: Epic Views of a Small Country* (Viking) and *Wales: The First Place* (Island Books)

The Estate of Rhys Davies for an extract from *Tomorrow to Fresh Woods*

The Estate of Glyn Jones for 'Again' and an excerpt from *The Valley, The City, The Village*

The Estate of Emlyn Williams and the Maggie Hoach Literary Agency for an extract from *George*

Mrs Glenys Ormond for *Johnny Randal* by John Ormond

Ronnie Knox Mawer and Bridge Books for a passage from *Land of My Father*

Siân James and Seren for an extract from *Storm at Arberth*

Gillian Clarke and Carcanet for 'Milk Horse' from *The King of Britain's Daughter* (1995)

J.M. Dent for *Llanrhaeadr ym Mochnant* and *The Green Isle* by R.S. Thomas

Iwan Llwyd for his own translation of *In Builth Wells – June 1988*

The Estate of Jack Jones and Hamish Hamilton for an extract from *Some Trust in Chariots*

The Felix de Wolfe Literary Agency for extracts from *The Stranger at my Side* and *A Welsh Eye* by Gwyn Thomas

The Estate of Gwyn Jones for passages from *The Mabinogion*, in his co translation with Thomas Jones

Professor Gwyn Thomas for *Bryn Celli Ddu*, translated by Joseph P. Clancy

An extract from *A History of Wales* by John Davies, reproduced by permission of Penguin Books Ltd

Marion Eames and Gwasg Gomer for an extract from *The Secret Room* in her own translation

John Davies and Seren for *Burying the Waste*

The University of Wales Press for an excerpt from *The Merthyr Rising* by Gwyn A. Williams (1978)

Christopher Davies Publishers Ltd for a passage from *The Master of Pen y Bryn*, translated by Nina Watkins

Rufus Adams for an extract from Lloyd George; *The Formative Years*, a booklet published by the WEA.

The family of the late R.G. Evans for part of a previously unpublished diary deposited in the Flintshire Archives Department

The family of the late R.G. Hughes for part of a previously unpublished diary deposited in the Flintshire Archives Department

Merryn Williams for a passage from *Border Country* by Raymond Williams

The family of the late Edna Gwynne Davies for diary extracts deposited in the Denbighshire Archives Department

Sally Roberts Jones for *Tryweryn*

Siân Preece and Polygon for an extract from a story contained in *From the Life*

John Idris Jones for *Aberfan*

D. Densil Morgan for an extract from an article in *The New Welsh Review*

Simon Farrington for an item from the *Western Mail*

Islwyn Ffowc Ellis and Gwasg Gomer for an extract from an essay included in *Artists in Wales* edited by Meic Stephens

The Estate of Saunders Lewis for an extract from *Buchedd Garmon* translated by D.M. Lloyd

Grahame Davies for his own translation of *On the Allotment*

12

John Barnie for an extract from his *Planet* article 'The Janus Country'

Raymond Garlick for an essay extract included in *Artists in Wales* edited by Meic Stephens, and also for his poem 'In the National Museum'

Dafydd Iwan for an extract from an essay included in *Artists in Wales* edited by Meic Stephens

Reproduced with permission of Curtis Brown Ltd, London, on behalf of the Estate of John Wain, an extract from *Winter in the Hills*, copyright John Wain 1970

David Greenslade for a sequence from his prose poem *Cambrian Country* (Gwasg Carreg Gwalch)

Myrddin ap Dafydd for *A Language is Only Words* translated by Tony Conran

R. George Thomas for *Offa's Dyke (Customs Office) 2000AD?*

Gladys Mary Coles for *Ancient Monument: St Non's at St David's*

Michael Ponsford; *Ffynnon Fair*

Enid Wyn Baines for *Glass*, translated by Gwynn Mathews

Joseph P. Clancy for *At Bala*

Ned Thomas for his co translation, with B.S. Johnson of *Glamorgan and Carmarthenshire*

Hutchinson for a passage from *Ukridge* by P.G. Wodehouse

Dr John Harris for passages from *Nothing to Pay* and *Taffy* by Caradoc Evans

Moira Dearnley for an extract from *That Watery Glass* (Christopher Davies, Publishing)

Herbert Williams for *Surfing*

The University of Wales Press for an extract from *How they Educated Jones* (1974)

Gwasg Gomer for the items listed below:
T.H. Parry Williams: *Llyn y Gadair*, translated by Joseph P. Clancy
Bobi Jones: *Llansteffan*, translated by Joseph P. Clancy

Cynan: *Aberdaron*, translated by Joseph P. Clancy

Waldo Williams; *St David's Day* and *On Weun Cas' Mael*, translated by Joseph P. Clancy

Menna Elfyn: *A Load of Coal*, translated by the poet

D.J. Williams: An extract from *The Old Farmhouse*, translated by Waldo Williams (Gomer)

T. Rowland Hughes: An extract from *The Beginning*, translated by Richard Ruck (Gomer)

Bloodaxe for 'The Other' by R.S. Thomas

Editor's Acknowledgements

I am most grateful to friends who have provided the stimulus which all anthologists need, and warmly thank Glenda Beagan, Siân James and Moira Dearnley.

My special thanks also to Joseph Clancy, who generously allowed me to draw on his vast output of translations, to Peter Howell Williams for drawing my attention to Macaulay's observations on Wales and to my publisher Myrddin ap Dafydd who commissioned the book.

Topography

People

History

Culture

Religion

Topography

Wales

Walking on the step of the shingle, here
Where the curlew follows the scallop of bay
And halts and prods the sand,
Looking beyond the cormorant's thoroughfare,
Beyond the drift and drip of the sea,
I saw the hills of Wales like stone clouds stand.

The sea flowed round them and the sky
Flowed under, and the floating peaks
Were frozen high in air;
I was a child then, and the winters blew
Mist across the skyline and spray against the rocks,
But blew open the window into Wales no more.

This year as a neighbour I looked at Wales;
Saw the sun on the rocks and the wind on the bracken,
And the telegraph poles like a boundary fence
Straddle the combe between the hills,
And westward from England and the Wrekin
Saw shadows of clouds advance.

But the sun was hot on the limbs, and the turf on the heels,
The berries were fat as grapes, and the way
Bent back on the Shropshire side of the border –
I walked no nearer Wales,
But returned to wait by the former sea,
Aware that the mist will never lift to order.

Norman Nicholson (1914-1987)

An Inventory

. . . the number is so great of sensible, educated men who have written about Wales, or would have written if business or indolence or dislike of fame had not prevented them, that either I find it impossible to visit the famous places . . . or, very rarely, I see that they were imperfect tellers of the truth . . .

Nevertheless, I will please myself and the discerning reader by repeating the names of a few of the places to which I have never been, or of which I will not speak, namely, Llangollen, Aberglaslyn, Betws-y-coed, the Fairy Glen, Capel Curig, Colwyn, Tintern, Bethesda, Llanfairfechan, Llanrhaiadr, Llanynys, Tenby, Mostyn, Glyder Fach and Glyder Fawr, Penmaenmawr, Pen-y-Gader, Pen-y-Gwryd, Prestatyn, Tremadoc, the Swallow Falls, the Devil's Bridge, the Mumbles, Harlech, Portmadoc, Towyn, and Aberdovey . . . I have read many lyrics worse than that inventory.

Edward Thomas (1878–1917):
Beautiful Wales

Eryri

I must not pass over in silence the mountains called by the Welsh Eryri, but by the English Snowdon, or Mountains of Snow, which gradually increasing from the land of the sons of Conan, and extending themselves northwards near Deganwy, seem to rear their lofty summits even to the clouds, when viewed from the opposite coast of Anglesey. They are said to be of so great an extent, that according to an ancient proverb, "As Mona could supply corn for all the inhabitants of Wales, so could the Eryri mountains afford sufficient pasture for all the herds, if collected together".

On the highest parts of these mountains are two lakes worthy of admiration. The one has a floating island in it, which is often driven from one side to the other by the force of the winds; and the shepherds behold with astonishment their cattle, whilst feeding, carried to the distant parts of the lake. A part of the bank naturally bound together by the roots of willows and other shrubs may have been broken off, and increased by the alluvion of the earth from the shore; and being continually agitated by the winds, which in so elevated a situation blow with great violence, it cannot reunite itself firmly with the banks. The other lake is noted for a wonderful and singular miracle. It contains three sorts of fish – eels, trout, and perch, all of which have only one eye, the left being wanting; but if the curious reader should demand of me the explanation of so extraordinary a circumstance, I cannot presume to satisfy him. It is remarkable also, that in two places in Scotland, one near the eastern, the other near the western sea, the fish called mullets possess the same defect, having no left eye. According to vulgar tradition, these mountains are frequented by an eagle who, perching on a fatal stone every fifth holiday, in order to satiate her hunger with the carcases of the slain, is said to expect war on that same day, and to have almost perforated the stone by cleaning and sharpening her beak.

Giraldus Cambrensis (c. 1146-1223)
The Journey Through Wales
Translated by Richard Colt Hoare

Llyn y Gadair

The jaunty passer-by will not see much
That's worth a look across its land-locked shoals.
More beauty in these mountains than in such
A scrap of lake, with nothing but the boat
Of a lone fisherman, flailing the water's skin
And rowing now and then from here to there
Like a bewildered wretch, or like a man
On nightmare deeps who cannot reach the shore.
But some magician with his hellish tricks
Has made me find a heaven in its face,
Although there is no splendour in its looks,
And on its banks there's no magnificence, –
Merely a peat-bog, its stumps dry with rot,
Two cliffsides, and two quarries long since shut.

T.H. Parry-Williams (1887-1975)
Translated by Joseph P. Clancy

Chepstow

Cats with sharp claws and nanny-goats in dread
Descend the shelving street and cautious tread.
What must we men then do to walk secure?
Observe the good old proverb – slow and sure;
For if we careless walk the slippery street
Our prostrate nether-ends the pavement greet;
And paying oft such honour to the stones
Will fix domestic prophets in our bones:
For when old bruises ache, they full as well
As corns and whip-cord change of weather tell.
But though in fear the street the stranger treads,
Within he'll find sure footing and soft beds;
The inns will furnish every want and wish,
For there he'll find good flesh, good fowl, good fish;
And those who on crimp salmon wish to feast,
In great perfection there will find it dressed.
Here is good ale, good cider and good wine
So that like sons of kings we here may dine.
In this snug town good meat and drink abound
But, strange to tell, there cannot here be found
One single inch of horizontal ground:
To social joys folks therefore here incline,
By way of exercise sit down to dine,
Grow plump and rosy, like the god of wine.

If strait the gate and narrow be the way
That leads from earth to realms of endless day,
Then through this town must be the road to heaven,
Whose gate is strait, streets narrow and uneven.
Such is the town of Chepstow, rugged, steep,
But a choice place to revel in, and sleep.

Edward Davies (1718-1789)
from *Chepstow: A Poem*

Not Without Regret

(The Whig historian Thomas Babington Macaulay stayed at Llanrwst for three months in 1821 on what became popularly known a few years later as 'a reading holiday'.)

I shall not leave Llanrwst without regret. It must be owned that it is a very dull place, that the uniformity of its events is diversified only by drunken battles, exhibitions of Jumpers, and fairs which keep every man who values his existence a prisoner to his rooms. At this moment one of these elegant scenes is going on. The streets are choked with pigs and calves, horses and horse-dealers, singing men and singing women, drunkards fighting, children screaming, cows lowing, and every now and then poking their heads in at my window to examine the furniture of my apartment. So much for the blessings of my Arcadia. Yet I shall, as I said, regret it, though I do not know why. I love every thing old and even when I have been accustomed to a place for three months only, I cannot part from it for ever without some concern.

Thomas Babington Macauley (1800-1859):
in a letter to his mother (1821)

A Journey Down The Border

My homeward journeys, often late at night, are nearly always unplanned and instinctive. Last year I was working on the North Wales coast, near Prestatyn. I finished in the early evening and decided not to stay for dinner. I paid my hotel bill and carried my bags to the car. I wiped the midges from the windscreen, sat in the car, fastened the safety belt, and went. I was going to make a fast run. It had been raining earlier, but the evening was brilliantly dry and sharp, the air washed clear. A few clouds moved out at sea, low on the skyline. I sat upright and relaxed, utterly at peace, knowing the extremities of the car as I knew my own skin, driving with the fingertips. I came down the Ruthin road, the A525, neatly and circumspectly, with an amused caution, knowing I could put the car wherever I liked, sensitive even to the grain of the road.

At Ruthin I turned off for Corwen and Llangollen. It was dusk, and a cold, erratic wind began to get up. Soon, before I reached Oswestry, I switched on the headlights. The road was empty. I went straight down the marches through Welshpool and Newtown before hitting the A44 at Crossgates. It was raining hard when I got to Kington. I stopped there and found a little coffeehouse still open, spoke a while with the sleepy young Italian waiter, and drifted gently out of town, the roads dark and wet. It was past midnight when I drove through Hereford. The heavy rain stopped as I was leaving the city. A policeman came out of a shop doorway, took off his wet coat, and shook it.

I knew where I was in general terms, but the darkness and the rain were making things difficult to recognize. I wanted to head for Gloucester through Peterstow and Ross-on-Wye, a road I've driven many times, but when I ran on to a long stretch of dual carriageway I knew I was lost. I wasn't worried. I knew I'd meet familiar roads soon enough. I pushed hard down the wide road, the car dipping gently as it met small pools of water at the edge of the drying surfaces. Two coaches passed, travelling in the opposite direction, their interior lights bright. I saw people asleep in their seats, their heads lolling against windows. The dual carriageway ended and with it the sodium lights overhead. I began to swing down the bends of a narrower road, the weight of sudden darkness oppressive. It was raining again. The car rocked like a boat through the washing gutters and I hunched my shoulders against the hills I felt were steep and close on either side. One or two houses, unlit and blank, stood at the sides of the road. Then I saw the river. I'm a sucker for rivers. I stopped the car and got out. Wind lashed the ends of my coat, the rain stung in its gusts. It was a lovely river; swollen by storms, ominous, full to the lips of its grass banks, its loud, black thunder rolled in the channels of my ears.

I got the big torch out of the car and walked down the road. The one street of a village slept under the whipped rain and I walked right through, to the far end. Then, on the left hand, a marvellous abbey pushed its ruined walls into the darkness, very Gothic, very romantic. I let the straight beam of the torch climb on its stones and arches. I knew where I was. I was in Tintern, on the banks of the Wye, looking at Tintern Abbey. A miracle of the night had brought me there. A single light came from a distant hill farm, hanging in the darkness a long way up. I watched it for a long time, wondering what emergency had called its people awake at two in the morning. It went out and I was left alone, listening to the loud river and the swift noise of the rain. I danced a little soft-shoe shuffle at the side of the road, in honour of William Wordsworth.

Leslie Norris: *Sing it Again, Wordsworth*
(A story included in 'The Girl from Cardigan') (1988)

Tintern

Five years have past; five summers, with the length
Of five long winters! and again I hear
These waters, rolling from their mountain springs
With a soft inland murmur. – Once again
Do I behold these steep and lofty cliffs,
That on a wild secluded scene impress
Thoughts of more deep seclusion; and connect
The landscape with the quiet of the sky.
The day is come when I again repose
Here, under this dark sycamore, and view
These plots of cottage-ground, these orchard-tufts,
Which at this season, with their unripe fruits,
Are clad in one green hue, and lose themselves
'Mid groves and copses. Once again I see
These hedge-rows, hardly hedge-rows, little lines
Of sportive wood run wild: these pastoral farms,
Green to the very door; and wreaths of smoke
Sent up, in silence, from among the trees!
With some uncertain notice, as might seem
Of vagrant dwellers in the houseless woods,
Or of some Hermit's cave, where by his fire
The Hermit sits alone.

William Wordsworth (1770-1850)
from *Lines Composed a Few Miles Above Tintern Abbey*

The view from Llandudno

The summer before last I spent some weeks at Llandudno, on the Welsh coast. The best lodging-houses at Llandudno look eastward, towards Liverpool; and from that Saxon hive swarms are incessantly issueing, crossing the bay, and taking possession of the beach and the lodging-houses. Guarded by the Great and Little Orme's Head, and alive with the Saxon invaders from Liverpool, the eastern bay is an attractive point of interest, and many visitors to Llandudno never contemplate anything else. But, putting aside the charm of the Liverpool steamboats, perhaps the view, on this side, a little dissatisfies one after a while; the horizon wants mystery, the sea wants beauty, the coast wants verdure, and has a too bare austereness and aridity. At last one turns round and looks westward. Everything is changed. Over the mouth of the Conway and its sands is the eternal softness and mild light of the west; the low line of the mystic Anglesey, and the precipitous Penmaenmawr, and the great group of Carnedd Llewelyn and Carnedd David and their brethren fading away, hill behind hill, in an aerial haze, make the horizon; between the foot of Penmaenmawr and the bending coast of Anglesey, the sea, a silver stream, disappears one knows not whither. On this side Wales – Wales, where the past still lives, where every place has its tradition, every name its poetry, and where the people, the genuine people, still knows this past, this tradition, this poetry, and lives with it, and clings to it; while, alas, the prosperous Saxon on the other side, the invader from Liverpool and Birkenhead, has long ago forgotten his.

Mathew Arnold (1822-1888)
On the Study of Celtic Literature

'Built to music . . . '

I went on, and was over the edge of this country, 'build to music and so not built at all', when the sun began to rise behind me. Before, a range of hills stood up against the cold sky with bold lines such as a happy child will draw who has much paper and a stout crayon, and looked so that I remembered the proverb which says, that if a man goes up Cader Idris at night, by dawn he is dead, or mad, or a poet. They were immense; they filled half the sky; yet in the soft light that felt its way glimmeringly, and as if fearfully, among their vast valleys and along their high crags, they looked like ruins of something far more mighty; the fields also, on this side of them, and all the alder-loving streams and mossy woods, were but as the embers of something which the night had made and had only half destroyed before its flight. And it was with surprise that, as I took my eyes off the prospect and looked down and in the hedge, I saw that I was in a place where lotus and agrimony and vetch were yellow, and the wild rose continued as ever to hesitate between red and white.

Edward Thomas (1878-1917)
Beautiful Wales

Llansteffan

How still is the plaitwork of seagulls above the castle
As though for a minute they'd grown into the sunshine.
There'll be need to practise the presence of seagulls
To keep their light flight when they are no longer here.
My stomach warms to them.
They turn on their enchanting wings against the breeze;
They row, like a river I want to dip my cup in,
And all its feathers flow for my delight.

Memory of a castle, memory of a village, memory of people
    watching birds
And the Tywi rhyming grief upon its sand:
They caress the chime of worship yet do not disturb it.
An old pretty village where the whole world comes to retire.

And one senses the smell of ruin in the service:
Over there, crows repeat the tail-end of their hymn,
The tame attachments of their grandfathers' tidy customs
Veering before the skeletons of the recollection of yesterday
And the people below (are they preachers?) citing English.

Pure joy to the seagulls like angels in flight through the village!
Do they foster the old nature of the spirits of the buried life?
The sun is the lonely soul on their wings.
In a long graceful tremor they rain in a low circle
To whisper purity to the contemporary debris,
A flash of comforts before they climb on the back of the blue.
Oh! let care be taken to practise the presence of seagulls
To keep their light flight when they are no longer here.

Bobi Jones (1929-)
Selected Poems. Translated by Joseph P. Clancy

A Rock Strewn Wilderness

East of Traeth Bach the hills of Meirionydd rise steeply, with a roll and pitch about Llyn Tecwyn and on and up to the flat tops of Mynydd Ysgyfarnogod and Clip. It is a lonely stretch with only a narrow coastal strip supporting life, from Harlech to Penrhyndeudraeth. As the ground rises through bracken to bog, rush and sphagnum, even the sheep thin out and a rock-strewn wilderness keeps a walker's pace down. It is a favourite area of mine. Any excuse will serve to take me there. At first the stream beds cut deeply back into a sort of plateau or flat-backed ridge, and the going is hard. But after the first seven or eight hundred feet the flat, broken plateau is reached and a rest is more than welcome. Beyond it the final ridges and folds rise more steeply still, but this long ridge under their shelter has its own separate identity, cut off by bog and stream from the surrounding wilderness and strangely hidden from the sea. This place must once have held importance in the eyes of our early forefathers. Hugging the southern end of this bare, concealed ridge lies the broken detritus of a strange monument. Invisible from the sea and the coastal strip, this monument is nevertheless clearly visible from the tops. Looking down it appears as a delicate circle, like a necklace laid on the flanks of mountain grass. The circular shape is not uncommon – the whole area bounds with circles – but this one is different, more perfect somehow and more delicate in plan. The reason for the relative delicacy is more readily seen as the monument is approached from the Harlech direction, where it suddenly appears against the sky, in profile. It is vaguely like a coronet, through only vaguely because it is made of rough, harsh, granite slabs, natural and undressed, all coruscated by the action of wind and weather. The rocks are long in shape, they point to the sky and, uniquely, they lean outwards, which accounts for the coronet appearance.

Jonah Jones
from an essay included in *Artists in Wales*,
edited by Meic Stephens

Green Man at the Bwlch

For a week or more
some baffling serendipity
has brought him to me
in books, journals, photographs –
a splay-mouthed face,
flesh shred with leaves.

Now on a remote pass above trees
of two Radnor valleys
I come to this ancient place –
cruck house half-crumbled, lovingly encased
by scaffolding and plastic sheets, cocoon
in which goes on the work of rebirth.
He is here too.

In a central room, on the beam
over the great hearth, royally
he spreads his mouth-borne branches,
meets my unsurprised eyes.
here is an abyss, like Nietzche's,
into which if I look long
I find it looking into me.

The terror is in his utter
neutrality. Yet somewhere
in his kingdom of possibilities
is a tree whose leaves give shelter,
whose boughs know songs, whose sap
flows gold through our veins.

Ruth Bidgood

A Paradise

These quaint cottages and inns, many of them built in the times of the Tudors and Stuarts, with their small windows and low, broad doors, with their low roofs, often of thatch, with their gardens of old-fashioned flowers and of vegetables at front and sometimes also at back, are utterly different from the conventional sameness and formality of modern streets, and recall ages more simple and spacious than our own. Man has placed them in all positions and at all angles; it seems more by accident than design that narrow passages have been left which we call streets by courtesy. There are many of these passages for so small a town, and it is easy for a stranger to wander round and round in them as in a maze, picking his way amid mud and puddles, amid ducks and chickens. Llantwit is a paradise for poet and artist, who would revel in its beauties and attractions, though it must be confessed that its cottages are frequently white-washed or yellow-washed externally, according to a very ancient custom of Glamorgan.

William Ewart Gladstone (1809-1898) in a letter.

Ode to Swansea

Bright town, tossed by waves of time to a hill,
Leaning Ark of the world, dense-windowed, perched
High on the slope of morning,
Taking fire from the kindling East:

Look where merchants, traders, and builders move
Through your streets, while above your chandlers' walls
Herring gulls wheel, and pigeons,
Mocking man and the wheelwright's art.

Prouder cities rise through the haze of time,
Yet, unenvious, all men have found is here.
Here is the loitering marvel
Feeding artists with all they know.

There, where sunlight catches a passing sail,
Stretch your shell-brittle sands where children play,
Shielded from hammering dockyards
Launching strange, equatorial ships.

Would they know you, could the returning ships
Find the pictured bay of the port they left
Changed by a murmuration,
Stained by ores in a nighthawk's wing?

Yes. Through changes your myth seems anchored here.
Staked in mud, the forsaken oyster beds
Loom; and the Mumbles lighthouse
Turns through gales like a seabird's egg.

Lundy sets the course of the painted ships.
Fishers dropping nets off the Gower coast
Watch them, where shag and cormorant
Perch like shades on the limestone rocks.

You I know, yet who from a different land
Truly finds the town of a native child
Nurtured under a rainbow,
Pitched at last on Mount Pleasant hill?

Stone-runged streets ascending to that crow's nest
Swinging East and West over Swansea Bay
Guard in their walls Cwmdonkin's
Gates of light for a bell to close.

Praise, but do not disturb, heaven's dreaming man
Not awakened yet from his sleep of wine.
Pray, while the starry midnight
Broods on Singleton's elms and swans.

Vernon Watkins (1906-1967)

Aberdaron

When I am old and honoured,
　With silver in my purse,
All criticism over,
　All men singing my praise,
I will purchase a lonely cottage
　With nothing facing its door
But the cliffs of Aberdaron
　And the wild waves on the shore.

When I am old and honoured,
　And my blood is running chill,
And watching the moon rising
　Stirs in my heart no thrill,
Hope will be mine thereafter
　In a cottage with its door
To the cliffs of Aberdaron
　And the wild waves on the shore.

When I am old and honoured
　Beyond all scorn and acclaim,
And my song goes by the rubric
　And gone is its passion's flame,
Hope will be mine thereafter
　In a cottage with its door
To the cliffs of Aberdaron
　And the wild waves on the shore.

For there I will discover
　In the stormy wind and its cry
Echoes of the old rebellion
　My soul knew in days gone by.

And I will sing with the old passion
  While gazing through the door
At the cliffs of Aberdaron
  And the wild waves on the shore.

Cynan (1895-1970)
Translated by Joseph P. Clancy

Secrets

Every landscape treasures its secrets. Children stumble across them without any immediate need to put them into words. Beyond the narrow belt of trees, above the sheep droppings and the clumps of gorse and limestone outcrops, there is a cave on the hillside that is equally suitable for prehistoric man, bandits, Indians, and schoolboys smoking their first cigarette. The school textbook says that in one 'chamber' of the cave fifteen skeletons were found closely packed together in a crouched position. A delectable, mute, mystery. And on top of the hill, the man-made tumulus is named Y Gop, where local legend persists in saying Boadicea is buried. A long way from home. What language did she speak? Dig our soil and you find eloquent oval cups, oak overlaid with gold, and thin breastplates for horses embossed and worked by hands that knew how to speak without words. The views from the hilltop are enticing, intoxicating. North-east lies the Wirral, where the Green Knight hides, mixing Celtic legends with Middle-English poetry. Westwards the white strength of Gwynedd, and the mountains rising like ramparts to touch the setting sun. From every point of the compass this unique landscape hides treasure trove. Even the impassive vastness of the level sea conceals sunken cities with secret histories, myths and legends.

To each mystery there must be a key: but the key of keys is the original language which hallows every hill and valley, every farm and every field with its own revered name. I must learn it and the more difficult it is the better. Hidden treasures like pearls and lost souls need to have their price. Cromlechs and chronicles, Celtic crosses and Roman mines, castles and chapels, wells, caves, coalmines and churches, ruined abbeys and choirs, 'the woods, waters, meadows, combes, vales / All the air things wear that build this world of Wales'.

Emyr Humphreys
from *Discovering Welshness*, (1993)
edited by Oliver Davies and Fiona Bowie

The River and the Road

The moon too has her times:
Last night
I was alone at the old bridge watching her at it,
Flinging into the swirling flood
Plate after white plate,
Recklessly smashing them all:
Each fragment giddily swimming a moment
Before sinking:
Then another,
And another.

When I turned from the bridge,
The moon was on the road:
She had now forgotten her mad prank at the river
And was pensively walking ahead of me:
Carefully, lovingly she picked up,
As if it had been a jewel,
Every bit of jagged flint
And the tiniest pieces of broken glass.

Wil Ifan (1882-1968)

Mysterious Britain

That gray morning I left you asleep
in the room overlooking Agincourt
Square, with the statue of King Harry
of Monmouth, and caught the bus to Trellech –
there being just one bus daily, and that one
so early there was no place to have breakfast
but a counter where regulars traded a patter
I couldn't make head or tail of – I was on the
scent of something a whole lot older
than Monmouth or the Battle of Agincourt.
The Wales of the Little People, a whiff
of huge unaccountable forces those
who are into the Craft believe they've
gotten in touch with.
               The bus – I was
its only passenger – wound upward
through beechwoods dazzling with holly
over a foot-thick purple carpet of
bluebells. Trellech was at the top,
overhung by a towering wizard's hat
of a spire: too wet a place (even in
hospitable Wales) to be quite friendly.
The Standing Stones I'd come thinking
would leap at me were so hard to find
I began to think somebody'd moved them.
But in fact they were where they'd
always been – lichened, leaning every
which way, in what was now a cowpasture.
Supposedly anyone coming too close, or with
unseemly intent, will be thrown back by
powerful oracular forces. Whether it's
true or not I can't say, I couldn't
get close enough because of the cows:
big Herefords, mythic nostrils
the size of caves, totem faces and
enormous rimmy eyelashes a frightful

milk-curdling white. I know cows
just enough to tell these weren't friendly.

There's a so-called Virtuous Well at
Trellech, clearly marked and such a cinch
to find, my guess is it's lost its virtue.
I'd intended to go back on foot,
get involved with holly and bluebells
if nothing else. But before I'd walked very far,
one of the hospitable Welsh came along in a
red sports car and offered me a lift.
There are some things, it seems,
you just can't get close to.

Amy Clampitt (1920-1996)

Carmarthen

Square Georgian houses wedged us in. Our front windows gave
upon a narrow street of them, superficially transformed into
shops, their plain façades and simple woodwork painted in sedate
tones. Lofty and impersonal, they seemed to impose upon us from
across the way, spurning the narrow muddy road, where rough-
hewn stones were strewn when the rains set in, to be crushed
down by the hoofs and wheels of a winter's traffic. When the rains
set in . . . but it was always raining. Children of the mist, we seem
to have passed from infancy to youth, from youth to adolescence,
enmeshed, immured in the fine reticulation of permanent rain. It
soaked into our clothes, seeped through our skins, penetrated our
lungs, our hearts, our brains. For weeks, for months, it would fall
day and night, softly, incessantly. The somnolent old town, the
wistful valley would be wrapt close in a vast blanket woven out at
sea by the warm south-wester. The clinging clouds might lift a
little, the valley reappear outlined in green and grey; then at either
end its lines would blur, they would fade out like thin green
flames before the reinvasion of sea-mist and more rain.

Always eager to overflow its banks, the sinuous river would creep out in pale sheets over the marshes and the vale become an arm of the sea thirty miles away when the windings were counted from its parent body. Soon the lower roads are covered; boats pass along with provisions; a plucky doctor's gig splashes through the mud. Dwellers on the quay have moved to their attic storeys whence, often enough, they watch their chattels swirl down-stream along with a carcass or two swept off the meadows. The modernised castle, used as a jail, looks the stern citadel it must often have been of old, riding an inland sea, now intercepted only by the parapets of the ancient bridge, sunk for the thousandth time beneath the flood.

P. Mansell Jones (1889-1968)
How They Educated Jones

Sheep in Blaenau Ffestiniog

The sheep in Blaenau stroll along the street.
When passing passers-by
they meet them squarely eye to eye,
don't blink or deviate – sure, the pavement
is wide enough for a sheep and a man –
though one looks like a proper gent,
the other Caliban.
The disdain of these sheep is exquisite.

Do sacred cows parade so royally?
Should we genuflect when they pass?
Could these unsheepish sheep enjoy
a liberty beyond us *hoi polloi*?

Ah, well . . . perhaps they go in search of grass,
and will find none in this vicinity.

Richard Poole

45

Return to Cardiff

'Hometown'; well, most admit an affection for a city:
grey, tangled streets I cycled on to school, my first cigarette
in the back lane, and, fool, my first botched love affair.
First everything. Faded torments; self-indulgent pity.

The journey to Cardiff seemed less a return than a raid
on mislaid identities. Of course the whole locus smaller:
the mile-wide Taff now a stream, the Castle not as in some black,
gothic dream, but a decent sprawl, a joker's toy façade.

Unfocused voices in the wind, associations, clues,
odds and ends, fringes caught, as when, after the doctor quit,
a door opened and I glimpsed the white, enormous face
of my grandfather, suddenly aghast with certain news.

Unable to define anything I can hardly speak,
and still I love the place for what I wanted it to be
as much as for what it unashamedly is
now for me, a city of strangers, alien and bleak.

Unable to communicate, I'm easily betrayed,
uneasily diverted by mere sense reflections
like those anchored waterscapes that wander, alter, in the Taff,
hour by hour, as light slants down a different shade.

Illusory, too, that lost dark playground after rain,
the noise of trams, gunshots in what they once called Tiger Bay.
Only real this smell of ripe, damp earth when the sun comes out,
a mixture of pungencies, half exquisite and half plain.

No sooner than I'd arrived the other Cardiff had gone,
smoke in the memory, these but tinned resemblances,
where the boy I was not and the man I am not
met, hesitated, left double footsteps, then walked on.

Dannie Abse

On Weun Cas' Mael

I walk once more on Weun Cas' Mael
As its gorse bushes, that never fail,
Declare that winter, withered and frail,
    Is losing the day.
'The blue of our bountiful sky will prevail,'
    Their faith's flames say.

And today at moments, clear and still,
Above the earth that's sodden, chill,
The skylark gives a lengthy trill,
    Bright song unchained,
True inspiration's trust and thrill,
    Hope of the land.

O! blossoms on the roughest plant,
O! song upon the steep ascent –
The same sweetness, from the same strength,
    The dear delight
Of bare acres that hide their worth
    From wordly sight.

O! Wales of the cairn and the dark moorland,
Nursery of independence of judgement,
Above the rubble your strength will stand
    From age to age.
Draw us to you: make us a part
    Of your life and ways.

In your grand austerity
You wakened men to charity,
Harmonious their society –
    Backed by your strength,
Their benign order flourished freely,
    With none a slave.

Waldo Williams (1904-1971)
Translated by Joseph P. Clancy

47

Llŷn

Skies tower here, and we are small.

Winters, we sleep on a flap of land
in a dark throat. We taste the salt
of its swallow. Huge cold breaths
hurtle over, cascade down
till we feel the house hunch.

Along the northern edge, the rocks
go on holding on
but taught obedience by ice, the clays
of the southern shore slide palely under.

When morning comes at last
houses sit up with pricked ears
on reefs of land the black tide
leaves, or sidle crab-wise
to the lane, their small squashed faces
giving nothing of their thoughts away.

In summer, flowers loosening with seed
reach out to fingerstroke
cars passing in the long sweet dusk.
Hay-meadows sigh. Pearl-pale
in the bracken on the headland
shorn ewes step delicate
and wary as young unicorns.

The sea we look out over is a navel
the wrinkled belly-button
of an older world: after dark
like busy star-systems, the lights
of Harlech, Aberystwyth, Abergwaun
wink and beckon. The sun's gone down
red as a wound behind Wicklow.
A creaking of sail away
Cernyw and Llydaw wait.

Once, here was where what mattered
happened. A small place
at the foot of cliffs of falling light;
horizons that look empty.
If we let ourselves believe it,
fringes.

Christine Evans

In Bardsey Sound

(Hilaire Belloc's 'The Cruise of the Nona' describes a journey by sea around part of the British coastline.)

I looked at the Carnarvonshire coast there close at hand, the sinking lines of the mountains as they fell into the sea, and I discovered myself to be for the first time in my life entirely indifferent to my fate . . .

Anyhow, here I was in Bardsey Sound, with many deaths moving over the howling fury of the sea, and not one of them affecting me so much as a shadow passing over a field.

The end of that adventure was odd and unreasonable – as things will be at sea. It was perhaps because we had been buffeted and pushed into some edge of the conflict between wind and water where the tide runs slacker; or it was perhaps because the wind had risen still higher. But, at any rate, after three separate raids forward (in the second of which we were very nearly out of our peril and into smooth water), and as many set-backs (one of which got us into the worst violence we had yet suffered) the *Nona*, in a fourth attempt (it was her own, not ours – we could do nothing but keep her, as best we might, to her course), slipped out and reached an eddy beyond the tide. For a moment it was very difficult to keep her to it, she slewed round; but then again she got her head southerly, and we found ourselves running past the great Black Rock which stands there – the Carrig Dhu – and marks the smooth water beyond the edge of the tide.

We breathed again; and as I took her on through an easy sea, close under the land with not too much strain upon the helm (for the high shore now broke the gale), I was free to look over my right shoulder and watch, passing away behind us, further and further, the hell of white water and noise, through which we had barely come to safety.

Danger keeps men awake and makes them forget necessity, but with this relief, our fatigue came upon us. My friend and I had now been awake for some twenty-five or twenty-six hours, and it was time for sleep.

We got the poor *Nona* which had behaved so well, up into a lonely little bay where was an old abandoned mine working, but no other sign of man. The Welshman with us told it was good holding ground; we let go the anchor and stowed sail. I remember how I fell half asleep as I stretched the cover over the mainsail boom and yard and tied it down at the after end. The gale still blew, yet, as it seemed, more steadily and less fiercely. There was no danger of dragging. We were well under the lee of the land. I gave one look, under the violent but clear morning sky, to seaward before I went below; and there I saw how, at a certain distance from the land, in a long line, the white water began. It was like being in a lagoon, like being protected by a bank from the sea outside; but really it was only the effect of the lee of the land making a belt of smooth water along shore. Then we all lay down to sleep and slept till evening.

Hilaire Belloc (1870-1953)
The Cruise of the Nona

A Solitary Walk

(The fictional output of George Gissing is largely autobiographical in one way or another. In 'The Whirlpool' he draws on a visit to Llŷn.)

In the sunny stillness their eyes wandered far and wide, around a vast horizon. On two sides lay the sea; to the west, bounded only where it met the blue sky above (though yonder line of cloud might perchance be the hills of Wicklow); eastward, enfolded by the shores of a great bay, with mountains on the far side, faintly visible through silvery vapour. Northward rose a noble peak, dark, stern, beautiful in the swift fall of curving rampart to the waves that broke at its foot; loftier by the proximity of two summits, sharp-soaring like itself, but unable to vie with it. Alone among the nearer mountains, this crest was veiled; smitten by sea-gusts, it caught and held them, and churned them into sunny cloudlets, which floated away in long fleecy rank, far athwart the clear depths of sky. Farther inland, where the haze of the warm morning hung and wavered, loomed at moments some grander form, to be imagined rather than descried; a glimpse of heights which, as the day wore on, would slowly reveal themselves and bask in the broad glow under crowning Snowdon.

The great silence had nothing of that awesomeness which broods in the mountain calm of wilder solitudes. Upon their ear fell the long low hushing of the wood, broken suddenly from time to time by a fitful wind, which flapped with hollow note around the great heap of stones, whirled as if in sport, and was gone. Below in leafy hollows, sounded the cry of a jay, the laugh of a woodpecker, from far heath and meadow trembled the bleat of lambs. Nowhere could be discovered a human form; but man's dwellings, and the results of his labour, painted the wide landscape in every direction. On mountain sides, and across the undulating lowland, wall or hedge mapped his conquests of nature, little plots worn by the toil or successive generations for pasture or for tillage, won from the reluctant wilderness, which loves its fern and gorse, its mosses and heather. Near and far were scattered the little white cottages, each a gleaming speck, lonely, humble; set by the side of some long-winding, unfrequented road, or high on the green upland, trackless save for the feet of those who dwelt there.

George Gissing (1857-1903)
The Whirlpool

Merioneth

. . . They now emerged, by a winding ascent, from the vale of Llanberis, and after some little time arrived at Bedd Gelert. Proceeding through the sublimely romantic pass of Aberglaslynn, their road led along the edge of Traeth Mawr, a vast arm of the sea, which they then beheld in all the magnificence of the flowing tide. Another five miles brought them to the embankment, which has since been completed, and which, by connecting the two counties of Meirionnydd and Caernarvon excludes the sea from an extensive tract. The embankment, which was carried on at the same time from both the opposite coasts, was then very nearly meeting in the centre. They walked to the extremity of that part of it which was thrown out from the Caernarvonshire shore. The tide was now ebbing: it had filled the vast basin within, forming a lake about five miles in length and more than one in breadth. As they looked upwards with their backs to the open sea, they beheld a scene which no other in this country can parallel, and which the admirers of the magnificence of nature will ever remember with regret, whatever consolation may be derived from the probable utility of the works which have excluded the waters from their ancient receptacle. Vast rocks and precipices, intersected with little torrents, formed the barrier on the left: on the right, the triple summit of Moëlwyn reared its majestic boundary: in the depth was that sea of mountains, the wild and stormy outline of the Snowdonian chain, with the giant Wyddfa towering in the midst. The mountain-frame remains unchanged, unchangeable; but the liquid mirror it enclosed is gone.

The tide ebbed with rapidity: the waters within, retained by the embankment, poured through its two points an impetuous cataract, curling and boiling in innumerable eddies, and making a tumultuous melody admirably in unison with the surrounding scene. The three philosophers looked on in silence; and at length unwillingly turned away, and proceeded to the little town of Tremadoc, which is built on land recovered in a similar manner from the sea. After inspecting the manufactories, and refreshing themselves at the inn on a cold saddle of mutton and a bottle of sherry, they retraced their steps towards Headlong Hall, commenting as they went on the various objects they had seen.

Thomas Love Peacock (1785-1859)
Headlong Hall

In the Valley of the Elwy

I remember a house where all were good
   To me, God knows, deserving no such thing:
   Comforting smell breathed at very entering,
Fetched fresh, as I suppose, off some sweet wood.
That cordial air made those kind people a hood
   All over, as a bevy of eggs the mothering wing
   Will, or mild nights the new morsels of Spring:
Why, it seemed of course; seemed of right it should.

Lovely the woods, waters, meadows, combes, vales,
All the air things wear that build this world of Wales;
   Only the inmate does not correspond:
God, lover of souls, swaying considerate scales,
Complete thy creature dear O where it fails,
   Being mighty a master ,being a father and fond.

Gerard Manley Hopkins (1844-1889)

A Pleasant Memory
(In the following letter extract, the poet and novelist John Wain writes to Dewi Roberts recalling a chance meeting in the Elwy Valley. Wain was in North Wales to deliver the annual lecture to the Gerard Manley Hopkins Society.)

What a pleasant memory that is, meeting you on the Saturday morning on that country road. Pat and I had taken a golden hour or so of leisure in a very busy day to get out into that very attractive landscape: we hadn't much time, but we couldn't possibly have put it to better use in that brief burst of glorious weather, amid rich new meadow grass, inquisitive cows, abundant wild flowers (more cowslips than Pat had ever seen growing wild) and that pleasant memory of meeting you.

John Wain (1925-1994)
in a letter to Dewi Roberts (1992)

Guy Fawkes Night
(for John Davies)

We Climbed above Prestatyn
  and paused for Breath,
  took in the full tide of townlights.
  Fireworks were shelling
  over flame-matted mounds,
  colours streaked and dripped.

On the sky's blacked out canvas
  a gibbous moon restored the wood's parting
  by Offa's Dyke,
  Openly showed us the border's old scar.

Clyde Holmes

Great Charm

The Welsh landscape has a great charm and when I see Snowdon
and the mountains in its neighbourhood, as I can now, with the
clouds lifting, it gives me a rise of the heart.

Gerard Manley Hopkins (1844-1889)
in a letter (1874)

People

The Ladies of Llanbadarn

Plague take the women here –
I'm bent down with desire,
Yet not a single one
I've trysted with, or won,
Little girl, wife or crone,
Not one sweet wench my own!

What mischief is it, or spite,
That damns me in their sight?
What harm to a fine-browed maid
To have me in deep glade?
No shame for her 'twould be
In a lair of leaves to see me.

No time was, but I did love;
Never so fixed a spell did prove
That natures like old Garwy's knew –
Every day, one or two!
For all this, I can go
No nearer than a foe.
In Llanbadarn every Sunday
Was I, and (judge who may)
Towards chaste girls I faced,
My nape to a God rightly chaste,
And through my plumes gazed long
At that religious throng.
One gay bright girl says on
To t'other prudent-prospering one –

'That pale and flirt-faced lad
With hair from his sister's head –
Adulterous must be the gaze
Of a fellow with such ways.'

'Is he that sort?' demands
The girl on her right hand,
'Be damned to him, he'll stay
Unanswered till Judgement day!'

O sudden and mean reward
For dazed love the brightgirl's word!
Needs I must pack my gear,
Put paid to dreams and fear,
And manfully set out
Hermit, like rogue or lout.
But O, my glass doth show
With backward-looking woe
I'm finished, I'm too late,
Wry-necked, without a mate!

Dafydd ap Gwilym (c.1325-c.1385)
Translated by Tony Conran

Dafydd ap Gwilym Goes To Town

Same Saturday night low expectations.
Why bother indeed
to powder the cock and pocket the lens case?
I don't even figure with the bus conductor
who stares right through me with his one good eye
and misses my fare.
Ah well, another quid
for the Double Dragon . . .

Too much boozing brings on dandruff.
Rosemary shampoo, they say, is a cure.
But I can think of a better one, cariad,
I can think of a better one.

Nigel Jenkins

The Last Blood

They were out, high on the hills. And there to the west lay Wales, folded in crumpled folds, goldish in the morning light, with its moor-like slopes and patches of corn uncannily distinct. Between was a hollow wide valley of summer haze, showing white farms among trees, and grey slate roofs.

'Ride beside me,' she said to Lewis. 'Nothing makes me want to go back to America like the old look of these little villages. – You have never been to America?'

'No Mam.'

'Don't you ever want to go?'

'I wouldn't mind going.'

'But you're not just crazy to go?'

'No Mam.'

'Quite content as you are?'

He looked at her, and his pale, remote eyes met hers.

'I don't fret myself,' he replied.

'Not about anything at all – ever ?'

His eyes glanced ahead, at the other riders.

'No Mam!' he replied, without looking at her.

She rode a few moments in silence.

'What is that over there?' she asked, pointing across the valley. 'What is it called?'

'Yon's Montgomery.'

'Montgomery! And is that *Wales* – ?' she trailed the ending curiously.

'Yes Mam.'

'Where you come from?'

'No Mam! I come from Merioneth.'

'Not from Wales? I thought you were Welsh?'

'Yes Mam. Merioneth *is* Wales.'

'And you are Welsh?'

'Yes Mam.'

'I had a Welsh grandmother. But I come from Louisiana . . .

. . . They came at last, trotting in file along the narrow track between heather along the saddle of a hill, to where the knot of pale granite suddenly cropped out. It was one of those places where the spirit of aboriginal England still lingers, the old savage England whose last blood flows still in a few Englishmen, Welshmen, Cornishmen.

D.H. Lawrence (1885-1930)
St. Mawr

Janet Ifans

Janet Ifans was an old woman who lived alone, a mile or two away from the town, in a little stone and slate cottage, perched like a toy over a dingle. Whenever she turned out the ash-pan it fell down two or three hundred feet to the torrent below, and everyone said that some day Janet would go with it. But she never did, and she died in her bed.

She was a very old woman with a light blue eye, a very wicked eye, and a shrill, high voice, which you could hear fields away, like a jay screeching. She was always shouting at the poor old donkey who was her only companion. His name was Ebenezer, but he was always called Ebbe. She was the widow of an old soldier in the South Wales Borderers who had died from wounds received in some foreign war, and the Dandy Fifth had a guard of honour when he went, and fired a round over his grave.

They were very happy together, except that on Saturday nights he used to unscrew his cork leg and beat her with it, but she did not seem to mind very much, and they were always in chapel again on Sunday billing and cooing like a pair of turtle doves. They had both come from somewhere down south, in the heyday of the little town, and Janet was a very vulgar woman indeed when she liked, though, as the sergeant had said, there was no harm in her, and she kept herself and the little house as bright as could be.

Every Saturday she went into the market with two baskets across the donkey, like panniers, filled with stuff from her little garden, and herbs that she sold in the town – mandrakes and dandelion roots, and such like. The journey in was easy enough, for it was downhill, but it was a different story coming back. And

58

every Saturday night Janet was drunk, her wisp of white hair blown across her face and her eyes wild, whacking the poor donkey across his rump and shouting abuse at him. He would trot for a few paces and then wait for her, and at the steep pitch she had to get her shoulder to him and give him a hoist up. And every Saturday he would always stop at the same place, with the old woman beating him with her umbrella, a crowd of little boys from the town behind her, shouting and laughing and throwing stones.

In the end people began to complain, because her language was very bad, but no one would do anything, for the old woman was ribald in her cups and she had a very quick wit. But when the Methodist minister intervened the story went round the town. She was a very strong Methodist, and she respected the cloth as nothing else in this world, but she was Janet Ifans, and that was all there was to it.

Geraint Goodwin (1903-1941)
The White Farm

Almost Holy

All the flags of July were waving; the sun and the poppies flaming; white butterflies spiring up and twining, and the bees busy on the snapdragons. The lime-trees were coming into flower. Tall white lilies in the garden beds already rivalled the delphiniums; the York and Lancaster roses were full-blown round their golden hearts. There was a gentle breeze, and a swish and stir and hum rose and fell above the head of Edward Pierson, coming back from his lonely ramble over Tintern Abbey. He had arrived at Kestrel, his brother Robert's home on the bank of the Wye only that morning, having stayed at Bath on the way down; and now he had got his face burnt in that parti-coloured way peculiar to the faces of those who have been too long in London. As he came along the narrow, rather overgrown avenue, the sound of a waltz thrummed out on a piano fell on his ears, and he smiled, for music was the greatest passion he had. His dark grizzled hair was pushed back off his hot brow, which he fanned with his straw hat. Though not broad, that brow was the broadest part of a narrow oval face whose length was increased by a short, dark, pointed beard – a visage such as Van-dyke might have painted, grave and gentle, but for its bright grey eyes, cinder-lashed and crow's-footed, and its strange look of not seeing what was before it . . .

A man of fifty, with a sense of beauty, born and bred in the country, suffers fearfully from nostalgia during a long unbroken spell of London; so that his afternoon in the old Abbey had been almost holy. He had let his senses sink into the sunlit greenery of the towering woods opposite; he had watched the spiders and the little shining beetles, the fly-catchers, and sparrows in the ivy; touched the mosses and the lichens; . . .

John Galsworthy (1867-1933)
Saint's Progress

A Most Delightful Confusion

. . . all trades and professions here lie in a most delightful confusion. The druggist sells hats, the shoemaker is the sole bookseller; if that dignity may be allowed him on the strength of three Welsh Bibles and the Guide to Caernarvon which adorn his window; – ink is sold by the Apothecary only; the grocer sells ropes (a commodity which I fear, I shall require before my residence here is over), and tooth brushes. A clothes brush is a luxury yet unknown in Llanrwst. When I asked for one, they brought me a stupendous old blacking brush which had been worn to the stumps on all the shoes and boots of, I suppose, half a dozen generations, and asked if that would do!

Still, I am contented, though I grumble. The people are harmless and quiet, and though ignorant, far from stupid.

Thomas Babington Macaulay (1800-1859)
in a letter to his mother (1821)

Adversity Overcome

If the place allotted to them to work was a good one and the rock easy to handle they could expect a low price, but since it was otherwise they could expect a much better price at the beginning of the month. But they were forced to accept this low price, and on top of it they all knew that the man who inspected the slates at the end of the month could discard more faulty ones when the market was weak.

Ifan often came home with three pounds for a month's work, sometimes four, and he considered taking home five pounds to be a very good wage. Once he took home just eighteen shillings after having worked hard for a whole month.

Until now Wiliam had had to depend on others for getting stones to work with, and he had no hope of anything better unless he could persuade some crew to take him on as a day labourer. But the day-wage man was paid so little that he would not be much better off after all. The only advantage would be that he would have a much better idea of what he was going to earn.

They were unable to repay any of the money they owed on the house. In fact, they were sometimes forced to borrow more money when it was necessary to buy a new cow after having had to sell the old one at a loss. They managed to raise enough pigs to pay the interest and the rates, but although Jane arranged to send six pigs a year to market instead of four by buying two porklings before the fatted ones had been sent away, she was not much better off. She had to pay more for pig meal, and she herself was far more tired at the end of the day.

It was true that Owen and Twm had won their schooling, but because the village, Moel Arian, was so isolated, it was an added expense to have to pay for the boys' lodgings during their last years at school. It would have been cruel to make them walk all the way home and then expect them to start on their ever-increasing amount of homework. They also needed better clothes and their books were expensive, although they received some grant towards these.

Wiliam and Elin were able to keep themselves – Wiliam failing sometimes – but Sioned never managed to do so. Her wages were not enough to keep her in food and clothes. But Jane Gruffydd managed to make enough clothes for Bet out of Sioned's old ones. When the mother wanted new clothes for herself – such as for the prizegiving – it meant getting deeper into debt.

She never saved on food. Unlike some others, she did not make a great effort to have butter to sell by putting less on the bread at home, or by mixing butter and margarine. She had one or two customers only, and these had their buttermilk free.

She worked morning, noon and night, doing the housework and most of the work with the animals. She made the children's underclothes and some of their outer garments. Before they went to the County School she would cut down Ifan and Wil's old trousers for Owen and Twm. She had little leisure for going anywhere or for reading. If she put on her spectacles to read in the evening, without fail she would fall asleep.

Her husband, too, was the same, toiling and moiling in the quarry; sweating and getting wet; coming home in the winter, wet to the skin, too tired to read a newspaper. In the Spring and Summer there would be work to do on the fields every evening and Saturday afternoon.

The only respite they had would be to get up later on a Sunday morning or to go to town occasionally on a Saturday afternoon. But they never grumbled about not having holidays; they would not know what to do with them if they had frequent ones. Their lot was to be eternally troubled and anxious about paying their way in the world, to keep out of debt, and acquire those things which they needed but wondered if they could afford.

But after earthing-up the potatoes or thatching the haystack, it was a great pleasure for Ifan to lean against the wall having a leisurely smoke while admiring the work of his hands, sometimes on his own, sometimes with a friend; to see the straight rows with the newly-turned earth around the dark shoots of the potatoes; to see the side of the haystack smooth and solid, and enjoy the sweet smell of the hay. So it was in the quarry when he had good stones which split cleanly and easily; he would sing as the work skimmed through his hands, and then the discussion in the shed after the mid-day meal. Yes, there was still some pleasure in life.

And at nightfall, placing his foot on the low wall at the front of

the house and letting his eyes rest on the sea which was red in the
setting sun, a feeling of quiet satisfaction would come over him.

Kate Roberts (1891-1985)
Traed Mewn Cyffion (Feet in Chains)
Translated by John Idris Jones and Idwal Walters

Taut and Gritty

In her old age Kate Roberts lived in Denbigh, and there a regular
stream of pilgrims went to visit her in her comfortable but oddly
incongruous 1930ish house, with its genteel lawns and mullioned
windows. She was very frail by then, and lay often upon her bed
almost unable to move: but so perversely wiry did she look down
there, so hard and grey, with her sharp quick eyes looking out of
her pain, and her hand resolutely on her walking-stick to heave
herself into a position of welcome – so taut and gritty was her
presence that it was rather like visiting one of her own stories,
seeing the sentences hewing themselves out before you, and the
hard attainment of adverbs.

Jan Morris
Wales: Epic Views of a Small Country (1998)

Doctor Price

Roderick shouted from the shop into the living-room one
afternoon: 'Hannah, come quick. There's old Doctor Price coming
up the road.'

The famous Doctor Price of Llantrissant! She hurried through
the shop and joined Roderick on the doorstep. As the news
travelled in the usual lightning way everybody was crowding out
of their houses. It was as if a king were arriving.

Slowly advancing up the sunny side of the street was a
dazzlingly venerable figure, attended on one side by a boy, the son
whom the strange old rebel had named Jesus Christ, and on the

63

other by his young daughter Penelope. Just over ninety though he was, Doctor Price carried his tall straight figure as even kings seldom do, and he wore his brilliant costume with a dignity that hushed laughter.

A white tunic of antique design partly covered his scarlet-and-gold waistcoat; his trousers were of green cloth with scarlet stripes and his green shoes of fanciful shape. More astonishing still was his headdress, which he declared was a symbol of healing. It was a whole bright fox-skin, the legs dangling like tassels about his shoulders, the long tail sweeping down his back. From under it came two long plaits of vigorous hair, silver as his tremendous beard. A faint pink was in the ivory of his cheeks, and his piercing gaze acknowledged with calm serenity the interest he was creating. His small grave son walked attired in a smaller fox-skin, a jacket of pale blue, and green knickerbockers. His equally grave daughter wore the traditional Welsh costume of tall black chimney-pot hat, red bodice and brightly checked flannel petticoats. They too were accustomed, like royalty, to taking their walks among an audience.

Rhys Davies (1901-1978)
Tomorrow to Fresh Woods

Courting

To court by day – to court 'in the face of the sun, the eye of light' – with no more modesty than the Gorsedd, is a recent thing in Wales. 'For they who wooed, wooed by night,' that is how it was with us, taking the girl from the fair or the eisteddfod or the auction or the cymanfa or the weekday meeting or making an appointment to go and 'knock' on her, on the window of her sleeping apartment, that was the custom, and if the wind was in the right quarter and all circumstances favourable you went into the kitchen quietly when every one else was in bed, and there you talked together on the hearth till the early hours of the morning. The official name for this was 'getting house'. A part of the charm of this courting was its pretence of being a secret between the two lovers. No one knew about it but themselves, as it were, just as a boy and girl sometimes are in love with each other on the quiet in a class in school (the teacher and the other children knowing nothing about it, of course!). The two would hardly even be seen together in public till they were on the verge of getting married – although everything was as plain to the world at large as if the banns had been called two years since. The tradition of courting in bed, if it ever had been a practice in the district, was gone before my time. Much nonsense has been written on this matter by people completely innocent of the art. What, indeed, was this love-making beside the naked calf-like kind which is met with to-day on every beach and bank?

Two suggestions may be offered as to why the Welsh people are the children of darkness rather than the children of light in their lovemaking. First a kind of sensitive shyness, half-romantic in its nature, that makes one feel there is in love a deep, mysterious component that would lose its sacred essence if it were displayed before the world. Like religion, love is a personal matter between two, and every one is not catholic enough to confess to a third person. They prefer to be *seceding* protestants. To the country-dwelling Welshman this love in public is a new phenomenon, and it must have come in either tamely on 'Santa Claus's' tail or with clamant obtrusiveness like Guy Fawkes. It seems like holding and exhibition. Although one might argue boldly to the contrary, much of the charm and inward delight of it was lost when we lost the old Welsh way. The other suggestion I make is that the stringent pressure upon people's lives in the old days kept every one at it assiduously from early in the morning till late at night, so that there was not much opportunity for social intercourse among young people except by stealing from the deep hours of the night. And as regards love in bed, wherever it might have been found, is it not enough to hold in mind the hard work on the farm during the day and the hard wood during the night on chair or bench or cushionless settle to realize how instinct and common sense might have suggested to two young people who were often pretty tired that they might rise a step in evolution by ascending to the room above and there resting on an easy bed, as the only place in the house where for a few hours they might find a degree of comfort,

however it might be as regards quiet? But Mrs Grundy's grave
face has never come back to place since she heard of this early fall
upward.

D.J. Williams (1885-1970)
The Old Farmhouse
Translated by Waldo Williams

Again

Lamplight from our kitchen window-pane
Shines out on the leaves of the little apple-tree
Dripping in the rain.

Inside the warm room, those two women together
Cleaning the brass candlesticks in silence
Are my daughter and my mother.

She has become a woman to me, my daughter,
Her dress heavy with her breasts, her arms heavy;
She is desired now, she is a lover.

But what will have come to her, and been hers,
Her crooked hands idle on the table
And her feet slow on the stairs?

Her granny, tired out, her mouth dropped open,
Sits with her eyes shut, facing the lamplight.
She has seen so much happen.

Shall my daughter too run through the streets to the pit-head,
And stand cold among the women crowding the gateway,
And see the young men brought up dead?

Glyn Jones (1905-1995)

Shouting at Nelson

Just before the death of Nelson, that great naval hero visited Merthyr; this was soon after the first Riots in 1800. He put up at the 'Star', where the cup out of which he drank is still (1907) preserved, and was there visited by the well-known Captain Jibb, of Dowlais, and another retired veteran named Will Ellis, who had formerly served under him. Nelson unexpectedly visited Cyfarthfa, and Richard Crawshay was so overjoyed at the honour that he wept. The introduction to the crowd was graphic. Richard seized Nelson by the hand, and turning to the great crowd, cried out, 'Here's Nelson, boys; shout, you beggars!' And they did shout! Two ladies accompanied him – one was Lady Hamilton. During the rejoicings which followed, an extemporised gun, made of a hollow bit of iron, burst, and wounded a boy fatally.

Charles Wilkins (1831-1913)
History of Merthyr Tydfil

Hills of Coal

Dear me . . . what would my father have done to me had he seen me smoking a cigarette outside Bethlehem Chapel? But I was telling you what a grand time was had by all in our hills of coal last Christmas. Oratorio on Boxing Night in the New Town Hall, Pantomime at our theatre, and on Christmas Eve prize drawings in all our public-houses. For your sixpenny ticket you had your chance of any of the following prizes:
A TURKEY
A GOOSE
A pair of FOWL
Joint of BEEF
Leg of PORK
Leg of MUTTON
A nine-gallon cask of best BEER
A bottle of WHISKY
A bottle of BRANDY

A bottle of RUM
A bottle of GIN
A box of CIGARS
– and some of our public-houses had a longer and better list of prizes than that!

Yes, a grand Christmas-time, yet not good enough to keep some of our young men in the hills of coal on Boxing Day. Hundreds if not thousands of them went on the trains to Cardiff, where they said they could see better football and enjoy themselves more so than at home.

Thanks to the way we have fed it with coal and iron and steel Cardiff is now the biggest town and port in Wales, and it has two theatres, one twice-nightly music-hall, two of those moving-picture places and a permanent waxworks show. And, worse luck, it has also got what we have never had, thank God, in our hills of coal. Bad gels who go with men for money, I mean. Pity, but there it is. Bad gels and their pimps and bullies, who prey on sailors in the docks area most of the time, but on a miners' holiday like Boxing Day and Night they leave that area for the main streets, on which they accost foolish young miners down for the day from our hills of coal. A strange place and an even stranger woman is a terrible temptation to young, unmarried miners down for the day from our hills of coal.

Jack Jones (1884-1970)
Some Trust In Chariots

Dedicated to Sadness

I clutched at my parents with my eyes – my hands were full of luggage – and thought, I must not lose sight of them, I shall be swallowed up in this eddy of faces and voices and houses and shops and footsteps, I cannot take it in I cannot . . . Shotton and Connah's Quay, merging into each other with indifference on both sides, were at that time a couple of hasty townships, wood and bricks and mortar run up at the behest of commerce; but on me, that busy Saturday, they had the effect of strong drink. Not only were the bicycles going quicker and ringing sharper bells, but the people with the preoccupied faces were walking brisker, the smoke from the strange houses blew faster, and even the town-clouds, brown at the edges from smuts and sophistication, raced swifter over a man-made sky. My head swam with the multiplication of fellow-beings, with the plurality of shops (ten in a row!) and with the danger of being lost. The swarthy old woman with the limp and the hat with a feather, swaying round a corner – had she gone for ever? Had I seen her? There was a man playing a cornet, for pennies, with a cap at his crippled feet, a man dedicated to sadness.

Emlyn Williams (1905-1987)
George

A Football Game
(*Wrexham*)

Like blood in veins,
the denim flood flows in the uniform streets,
in red and white corpuscles
of the tied scarves and woollen hats
into the heart of the town.

In eager liquid,
they pour,
from Cefn and Acrefair,
from Penycae and Rhos,
from Brymbo and Broughton and Llay,
into the lungs of the Racecourse.

Here, on a woman-less Wednesday night,
the blood and breath of these parts
beats and trembles,
in the two-hour strength of the mass body,

and the energy of the one hoarse voice
drives the ball, like meaning,
into the net of the understanding.

And after the game,
the turning into the night;
like blood in veins,
the denim flood flows in the uniform streets,
from the heart of the town,
from the lungs of the Racecourse,
to the far reaches of the neighbourhood.

And after the strength of the belonging,
Wrexham Rule, OK?

Bryan Martin Davies
Translated by Grahame Davies

Johnny Randall

When the moon was full (my uncle said)
Lunatic Johnny Randall read
The Scriptures in the dead of night
Not in bed by candlelight
But in the field in the silver glow
Across the lane from Howells Row;
And not to himself but to the sheep
With the village barely fallen asleep
And colliers who'd worked two-till-ten
In no fit shape to shout *Amen*
Grumbled *The bugger's off again.*

He'd dip in Chronicles and Kings
Dig into Micah, Obadiah,
Lamentations, Jeremiah,
Ezekiel, Daniel, on and on
Into the Song of Solomon:
A great insomniac heaven-sent
Digest of the Old Testament,
Faltering only in his loud
Recital when a pagan cloud
Darkened the Christian moon and bright
Star congregation of the night.

Then Johnny Randall in a vexed
Improvisation of the text
Would fill in with a few begats
Of Moabs and Jehoshaphats
(Windows banged shut like rifle-shots)
And Azels, Azrikans and all
The genealogy of Saul,
Till David's line put out new shoots
That never sprang from royal roots,
And wombs long-barren issued at
The angel seed of Johnny's shouts.

When clouds veered off the moon's clean rim,
Another chapter. Then a hymn
To close the service. So he'd sing

In the big deeps and troughs of sin
No one lifts up my drowning head
Except my bridegroom Jesus Christ
Who on the Cross was crucified . . .

Then silence. Benediction: *May*
The Love of God and
The Fellowship of the Holy Spirit
Be with you always
Till the great white moon comes again.

Stillness. Until at last
Johnny would rouse himself
And take up collection from the cows.

John Ormond (1923-1990)

Uncle Gomer

It is our Llansant fair-day, but early, the window-blinds are still down, the black heavily-beaded house-doors opposite still bolted, like rows of life-size portraits tarred all over, frames and all. With my head out of the pointed window I hear the dissonant scraping of a heavy bucket on cobblestones, and the pigeons billow up as my Uncle Gomer appears in the sunshine at the front of the house, the halting obliquity of his bearing exaggerated by the weight of his one-handled burden. An eggy-beaked blackbird flees, scalded and screaming, below me as he approaches, but the fountainous pigeon flock recognizes him and subsides.

I wait to hear his latest story. Yesterday the body of a young man drowned up at Tremyrddin was said to have been seen in the river above Llansant, so he has a new tale to tell. Gwydion meanwhile stirs in the wool behind me and his bed creaks with its contents; while Nico, awakened, clowns, and lances his inappropriate canticle into the morning. Ancestry has endowed him with the thorax and vocal organs of the *basso profundo*, but he can counterfeit the exalted registers of the castrati and man-sopranos. He now does so and his hymn, to the tune of 'Les commandements de Dieu,' is, 'The day Thou gavest, Lord, is ended'.

My Uncle Gomer, hearing Nico's falsetto, looks up, sees my head projecting under the boarding-house blue of the eaves and greets me with a good morning which I return. Even now, bearing boiled chicken-meal, the grey rings cling thick about his elegant skull with the perfection of ornate masquerade hair. His long and princely face, although unshaved, although rugged and elaborately wrinkled with a mobile webwork of grooves, fine lines, and creases, is handsome-boned, is fleshed with arched nostrils, and thick brows delicately canted outward. During momentary respite his features are benign, contemplative, and hierophantic, but always in his brown eyes he has the sparkle of a star.

Glyn Jones (1905-1995)
The Valley The City The Village (1956)

Miss Pritchard

It was freezing cold in Miss Pritchard's classroom. Gordon Rees, Donald Jenkin and Arthur Ffoulkes all managed to find space in the desks next to the hot water pipes running along the wall.

'Take out your books,' called Miss Pritchard. She spoke in a harsh North Wales accent and was known locally as 'a bit of a Nashie.' This was a reference to her activities with the Welsh Nationalist Party. Miss Pritchard wore a Fair Isle knitted cardigan over a bunched tweed skirt. The lace collar of her blouse was kept in place by a mysterious badge depicting a crossed leek and dragon. Underneath was a slogan in Welsh which I did not understand. According to Gordon Rees it meant 'Bugger the English' but Aunt Carrie said Gordon was 'a common boy' so I was careful not to mention the subject at home.

'Books out,' said Miss Pritchard. 'The famous poems which you have to learn by heart are I'm afraid all by English poets. But of course it was the glories of North Wales that gave them the necessary inspiration for their greatest works.' She was just about to turn towards the blackboard.

'Now don't tell me, Ronnie Knox Mawer' she said through her projecting teeth. 'You've lost your book already!' With some reluctance, I drew out my brown paper-covered exhibit. From the adjoining desk Gordon Rees began to snigger.

'He's got his dad's shop window cut out on the front,' he whispered to Arthur Ffoulkes.

'More like a bloomin' Punch and Judy show' Arthur agreed. I felt myself blushing scarlet. Once again, Father had conspicuously refused to conform. Fortunately, their attention was distracted.

'Hail to thee blithe spirit,' called out Miss Pritchard. 'Bird thou never wirt' Miss Pritchard was facing us now. With large bony hands, she clasped the book to her breast, eyes heavenwards.

'Higher still and higher,' she continued 'from the earth thou springest like a cloud of fire!' By this time, the novelty was wearing thin. Gordon Rees kept a box of matches in his trouser pocket. A daring boy, he was well known for his practical jokes. I watched in horror as he put a light to a screwed-up piece of lavatory paper.

'Watch out Knoxy,' Gordon hissed 'there's a bloomin' cloud of fire under your b.t.m.' It so happened that Dorothy Emlyn was a somewhat incontinent child. On this occasion, her nasty little habit of producing a pool of water under the desk proved useful. Miss Pritchard was too far gone to notice anything amiss.

'Teach us, sprite or bird,' she continued 'what sweet thoughts are thine.' She paused to draw breath.

'Can I be excused Miss Pritchard?' whispered Dorothy Emlyn.

'About bloomin' time,' said Gordon Rees behind his hand. Miss Pritchard closed the book.

'The first two verses to be learned as homework' she said. She turned to me. 'Perhaps your father will take you on a trip to where Shelley wrote his poetry!' I sensed that Father was singled out in this way because Miss Pritchard had what Aunt Carrie called 'a soft spot' for him. When Father, as a school governor, had paid an official inspection, I had overheard her say to Miss Powys (Infants), 'Fine figure of a man isn't he?'

Now however, it was Mr Shelley 'the great Radical' as she called him who was foremost in Miss Pritchard's mind.

'No need, I hope, to emphasise yet again,' she said to me 'that the poet's finest work was inspired here. In North Wales.'

'Here, Miss Pritchard?' I questioned. A colliery chimney was belching out thick smog over the slag heap, engulfing the playground.

'That,' she snapped, 'is the defilement of our Nation by English Capitalism.' She closed her eyes. 'I am referring to the glories of the mountain scene at Tremadoc where Shelley took his young wife for a blissful period of creative activity.'

As it turned out Father did not respond kindly to the idea of a Shelley Excursion. He took the Anthology from my hand and turned to the page where the poet was depicted.

'A dangerous revolutionary' he declared. 'You can tell from the slovenly way he dresses!' The poet was depicted in a loosely fitting white shirt, worn open at the neck with a crumpled cravat. The very sight of such an outfit was anathema to Father's sense of propriety. 'From what I gather the man was nothing but a wastrel,' Father said.

Ronnie Knox Mawer
Land of my Father (1994)

Pastoral

This morning, yawning, Dic Fawr said
'Evans the "Ship and Castle" is dead'
'Is he indeed? Poor chap,' I said.

The huge horse rose in its shadowy stall
We smoked and watched its brown excreta fall
And Dic, said, spitting 'After all

You couldn't expect a chap like that
With bottles to hand from where he sat
Not to soak. His belly was like a vat.'

Dic went across to stir the horse's feed.
'Come on, Eat up,' he said, 'you're harrowing the fifteen acre field
All day today,' and wistfully to me, 'It was a nice death indeed.'

Outside the lark was gargling with dew
When Dic led out Captain Bell and True
The sunlight dripped in the lane. The sky was blue.

Emyr Humphreys

Glyn Parry of Llanddu

Miss Morris sat with her hands in her lap and remembered her
sweetheart, Glyn Parry from Llanddu, who'd been killed in Burma
nearly fifty years before. She seldom thought of him now; his
memory, a half-forgotten tune, only occasionally disturbing the
surface of her mind.

Her parents hadn't approved of him. She was too good, they
said to marry into the haulier business; she with the County School
behind her and all the money they'd spent on her piano lessons.

But she would have married him, all the same. If he'd come
back.

He was tall, round-shouldered because of his height and his

job, with a large, shaggy head and sad blue eyes. He was too shy to arrange meetings, he'd just turn up from time to time; outside the library at five o' clock on a Saturday afternoon or occasionally after chapel on a fine summer evening.

She remembered with shame how she'd once berated him because he never let her know when she could expect him, and how he'd blushed and mumbled about the nine miles he had to cycle – no distance he'd said, except after heavy rain when the mile-long farm track from their house was muddy and almost impassable. You musn't come so often, she'd said, then, and he'd smiled the nice slow smile that changed his face.

They'd walked on the hills in the summer, gone to the cinema, whatever the film, in the winter and rough weather.

What had they talked about? Nothing much that she could remember; her job in the library, her parents, his parents and brothers and sisters – none of whom she'd ever met – places he'd gone to that week in the lorry. They liked the same programmes on the wireless. When she listened to the poetry contest on a Tuesday evening or to the play on a Wednesday, she liked to think that he would be listening too, and that they would discuss them – or at least she would, he never said much – when they'd next meet. They never talked about love.

The love in their affair had only begun after he'd been called up and sent to England to begin his training. Then his letters had been full of his longing for her. Things he had never dared to speak, he wrote with an ease and fluency that surprised her. He agonised about all the kisses he had never given her for fear she would repulse him. 'I didn't dare hope,' he wrote, 'that my feelings for you would be returned.'

'They are returned,' she confessed in her reply, trembling at the strength of them. 'I love you and I'll wait for you.'

A few months and many letters later, he'd sent her an engagement ring, a narrow gold band with three tiny diamonds and she'd worn it in spite of her mother's disapproval. 'Your father gave me a solitaire,' her mother'd said with a sniff. 'Why couldn't you get yourself a bank-clerk or a teacher? Throwing yourself away, that's what you're doing, you with your French and your German, never mind your piano.'

All the same, he'd been invited to the house when he came home for his first leave.

Her mother had made an elaborate meal, with knives and forks laid out in pairs like in a hotel; she was sure it was only to embarrass him. It had been an awkward evening, but they'd survived it, and afterwards she'd taken him out as far as the gate and he'd kissed her, though not as ardently as he did in his letters.

And within another six months he was sent to India and before the end of the year he was dead.

And she'd gathered together all his precious letters and momentos and had burned them in the garden. It had been like a memorial service for him, with her the only mourner.

Siân James
Storm at Arberth (1994)

Milk-Horse

News in the post of a birth
– easy and slippery –
and the difficult dying of friends,

to the knock knock
of fence-posts, chiff chaff, hoofbeats
and the hauled load of a milk-horse
forty years ago,
ears flattened and hooves slipping
on the steep half mile between yard and gate,
milk askew in the churns
and the leather cold as a knife.

Two girls, then,
one urging a little mare up a glassy lane,
the other elsewhere, dreaming
the still untravelled continents
of her school atlas,

the galleries, the cool churches locked
in its glowing pages.

Two women, now,
one here at the window
open on the May garden
reading news of a birth, a death, a dying,
the other far away in her hospital bed
hauling herself slowly, slowly
over the stones of the day.

Gillian Clarke

The Green Isle

It is the sort of country that,
After leaving, one is ashamed of
Being rude about. That gentleness
Of green nature, reflected
In its people – what has one done
To deserve it? They sit about
Over slow glasses, discussing,
Not the weather, the news,
Their families, but the half
Legendary heroes of old days:
Women who gave their name
To a hill, who wore the stars
For bracelet; clanking warriors,
Shearing the waves with their swords.

That man shuffling dustily,
His pants through, to the door
Of the gin shop, is not as mean
As he looks; he has the tongue
For which ale is but the excuse
To trespass in golden meadows
Of talk, poaching his words
From the rich, but feasting on them
In that stale parlour with the zest
And freedom of a great poet.

R.S. Thomas (1913-2000)

Uncle Edwin

Sometimes when you mentioned to my Uncle Edwin the many grave flaws in man's condition on this earth he would burst into tears. Even in Windy Way where we lived and where the tear gland is often found to be as muscled and articulate as a third arm a man needs a lot of working on to reach this state.

When Teilo Dew, who talked often at the Discussion Group which met at the Library and Institute in Meadow Prospect, said that the world was the mere rear side for the whole universe, his friend Milton Nicholas said that if it were so then Uncle Edwin should be given a medal of beaten lint as the leading boil upon this rear, so touchy and blown upon by the long winds of pity was he.

Uncle Edwin was not brought to this high state of finish swiftly or without care. In the Tonypandy riots into which he had dropped only as a visitor and an amateur of tumult in all its shapes and forms he had stuck his head in the way of conflict and had a baton broken over it by a policeman who hated short strikers and long batons and liked making the first taller by a whole lump and the latter shorter by as much as the strikers were willing to have snapped off over their heads. The policeman said that in these respects Uncle Edwin had been one of the most satisfying voters he had ever dealt with. The blow kept my uncle's head singing for seven years and they say it was very pleasant on winter nights to have his head bones twanging out the simpler tunes in the quiet of the kitchen with the various elements who called in to see Uncle Edwin bending forward on their seats around the room contributing the uncanny harmony of voice and mood for which Windy Way has always been renowned. He even entered his head for four eisteddfods to do a bit of chanting scored for one skull and a bitter heart but on each occasion he was disqualified for subversive subtlety. The singing died down during the first great strike of 1921 when his head noises went to join the deep sense of wonder and stillness that fell upon us all.

Gwyn Thomas (1913-1981)
The Stranger at My Side

Instructing-the-natives

In the by now unhallowed Freudian manner I remember first realising why girl-friends tended to demur when invited to 'the pictures' at *The Empire*. Girls preferred the better 'policed' *Majestic Cinema*, where usherettes were inclined to subdue and sometimes eject noisily wrestling couples going in for some energetic sexual karate in the back two rows. One night at *The Empire*, which was, incidentally, the first of the three cinemas Caernarfon then sported to succumb to the Bingo-bacillus, a fact which may have saved the building from demolition, seated stiffly beside a very quiet girl given to the occasional Cassandra-like utterance ('We'll *burn* to death in here. I can't see a fire-exit', she had muttered on the way in) both of us islanded in an urgently, whispering, groping undergrowth of squeaks, grunts, gasps and the plangently oily pong of Brylcream, I discovered that cinema's covert attraction for males. I eyed my companion hopefully and squintingly but nothing happened. Her attention was glued sombrely on the screen. Perhaps she was exclusively a connoisseur of the macabre. I should have had fangs.

When we were younger we used to go to Saturday matinees at *Y Maj* (The Magestic) and sit, sometimes in stunned, vaguely resentful silence or loud scorn as, prior to the inevitable Western, we watched a little white dot bounce, in emphatic synchronicity with the tune, idiotically along the words of songs like 'I've got sixpence, a jolly, jolly sixpence'! Who wrote that subtle piece of propaganda, I wonder; some earnest lyricist? You were blessedly lucky if you had one – a whole *sei!*[1] The songs were generally tunes like 'Roll out the barrel', 'I've got a luvverly bunch of coconuts', 'The White Cliffs of Dover' (Where was Dover?) and, once or twice, probably by an error soon corrected when it reached the permanently pricked ears of Those Who Know Best, 'Roll me o-ver, in the clover/Roll me over, lay me down and do it again!' and other pearls. The voice-over seemed to have been dredged from a four-ale bar in deepest Fulham. There was an air of Instructing-the-natives in such features, rather like one fancied some crude propaganda-drive would be.

[1] Caernarfon slang for sixpence.

Peter Gruffydd
Damned Braces
his early autobiography, included in
'The New Welsh Review' (1994)

In Builth Wells – June 1998

They're my own people, this crowd
in the karaoke tavern on country music night,

Mr Blobby dancing
with the middle-aged blonde who accused me

of being depressed,
who asked me to dance, me as out of place

as a midwife at a funeral, uneasy as a thief in court precincts,
wondering if I'd get out alive

groping for my excuses, yet wanting to cross the bridge,
because these people are as necessary

as the dew-faced Urdd children,
singing their Dafydd Iwan songs,

more necessary, in their rhinestone shirts
and El Alamo shoes:

so I keep on dancing
and listen to what the karaoke says:

it says Tina Turner has found the secret of how to be free,
and they are impersonating her,

searching their language to voice their own freedom:
and sometimes a marriage comes from this endless dance,

and sometimes a death.
Remember, this is the Cilmeri of the corpses.

Iwan Llwyd
Translated by the poet

History

Bryn Celli Ddu

(Bryn Celli Ddu is an ancient burial mound in Anglesey. It is thought to date from c.2000-1500 BC.)

Amid earth and rocks, like an old dog,
Death was gnawing on a bone
Three thousand years at Bryn Celli Ddu.

Till the sun was hacked into its belly
And time shovelled from the skeletons
And grey echoes of a race's early life laid bare.

There was no sound of mortality scuttling
Grossly, horribly, angularly among the stones;
In the analysing of the darkness it left there quietly.

And those who once walked Môn, their quality went
Through the earth, green to the grass and bright to the water,
Their lives were washed by the rain, the sun drank up their pain.

Their life went astray in the wind,
Was lost in the long time
Stretching between us and what used to be.

But their being is in our blood,
A crimson secret pumping through our hearts,
A bond of living, a grasp of recognition.

And such poor things as we
Against the muddled strength of death
Pierce the grave's armour with our ancestors' remains.

Gwyn Thomas
Translated by Joseph P. Clancy

The Arrival of Matholwch

('The Mabinogion' is a medieval text which consists of twelve tales from various parts of Wales. The story of the ill-fated Branwen opens at Harlech when Matholwch, the king of Ireland, arrives to claim Branwen's hand in marriage in a symbolic gesture to unite Britain with Ireland.

For the first year of the marriage they were happy, but their union was disrupted when old grievances between the two countries were rekindled and Matholwch's brothers decided to settle these old scores. As a result Branwen was humiliated by being forced to work in the kitchens. She managed to rear a starling and taught it to say her name. She then told it to fly back to Wales in order to find her brother, Bendigeidfran. When he learned of the circumstances in which his sister found herself he was enraged and with his fleet of ships set off across the Irish sea. In the battle which resulted much blood was spilled and there were only seven survivors. Branwen herself was able to return to Wales where she died of grief.

This is the opening of this tragic story.)

Bendigeidfran son of Llŷr was crowned king over this Island and exalted with the crown of London. And one afternoon he was at Harddlech in Ardudwy, at a court of his. And they were seated upon the rock of Harddlech overlooking the sea, and his brother Manawydan son of Llŷr with him, and two brothers on the mother's side, Nisien and Efnisien, and besides these, noblemen, as was seemly around a king. His two brothers on the mother's side were sons of Euroswydd by his mother Penarddun daughter of Beli son of Mynogan. And one of those youths was a good youth; he would make peace between the two hosts when their wrath was at the highest: that was Nisien. The other would cause strife between the two brothers when they were most loving.

And as they were seated thus, they could see thirteen ships coming from the South of Ireland, and making towards them with an easy swift motion, the wind behind them, and nearing them swiftly. 'I see ships yonder,' said the king, 'and making boldly for the land. And bid the men of the court equip themselves and go and see what their intent is.' The men equipped themselves and approached them below. When they saw the ships from near at hand, certain were they that they had never seen ships in fairer trim than they. Beautiful, seemly, and brave ensigns of brocaded silk were upon them. And thereupon, lo, one of the ships outstripping the others, and they could see a shield lifted up above the ship's deck, with the point of the shield upwards in token of

86

peace. And the men drew near them that they might hear each other's discourse. They put out boats and came towards the land, and they greeted the king. For the king could hear them from the place where he was, upon a high rock over their heads. 'God prosper you,' said he, 'and welcome to you. Whose is this host of ships, and who is chief over them?' 'Lord,' said they, 'Matholwch king of Ireland is here, and the ships are his.' 'What would he?' asked the king. 'Does he wish to come to land?' 'Not so, lord,' said they, ' – he is come on an errand to thee – unless he succeed in his errand.' 'What errand is his?' asked the king. 'He seeks to ally himself with thee, lord,' said they. 'He has come to ask for Branwen daughter of Llŷr, and if it seem good to thee he wishes to unite the Island of the Mighty with Ireland, so that they become the stronger.' 'Why,' he replied, 'let him come to land, and we will take counsel concerning that.'

The answer went to him. 'I will go gladly,' said he. He came to land, and he was made welcome, and great was the throng in the court that night, what with his hosts and those of the court. Straightway on the morrow they took counsel. What was determined in council was to bestow Branwen upon Matholwch. And she was one of the Three Matriarchs in this Island. Fairest maiden in the world was she.

The Mabinogion
Translated by Gwyn Jones and Thomas Jones

A Letter From Camp

(This letter was written by a knight in the service of Henry III during a period when a war was being waged with the Princes of Wales. The dreadful conditions of Mediaeval warfare are graphically conveyed here. The castle concerned is the one at Deganwy, of which scarcely anything exists of even the ruins today.)

September 24th, 1245

His Majesty the King, with his army, is encamped for the purpose of fortifying a castle which is now built in a most strong position;

and we are dwelling round it in tents, employed in watching, fastings, and praying, and amidst cold and nakedness. In watchings through fear of the Welsh suddenly attacking us by night; in fastings, because of a deficiency of provisions, the half-penny loaf being now risen to five pence; in prayings, that we may soon return safe and scot free home; and we are oppressed by cold and nakedness, because our houses are of canvas, and we are without winter clothing. There is a small arm of the sea which ebbs and flows under the aforesaid castle (where we are staying), and forming a sort of harbour, into which, during our stay here, ships have often come from Ireland, and from Chester, bringing provisions. This arm of the sea lies between us and Snowdon, where the Welsh quarter themselves, and is, at high tide, about a crossbow-shot wide. On the Monday next before Michaelmas, in the afternoon, a ship from Ireland, bringing provisions to us for sale, was coming up towards the entrance of the harbour, but, being incautiously steered, as the sea receded, it remained aground under our aforesaid castle, but on the opposite bank, towards the Welsh, who immediately rushed down and made an attack on it as it lay on the dry ground. We, therefore, seeing this proceeding from the bank on this side, sent three hundred Welshmen, our borderers from Cheshire and Shropshire, across the water, in boats, together with some crossbow-men, to defend the said ship, on seeing which the Welsh hurriedly retreated to their accustomed and well-known hiding-places in the rocks and in the woods. Our knights, attended by their followers, pursued them for a distance of two leagues, and although they were on foot (for they had not brought their horses across the water with them), they wounded and slew many of the Welsh. Our people then returned, after defeating their enemies, and, like greedy and needy men, indulged in plunder, and spread fire and rapine through the country on the other side of the water, and, amongst other profane-proceedings, they irreverently pillaged a convent of the Cistercians, called Aberconway, of all its property, and even of the chalices and books, and burnt the buildings belonging to it. The Welsh, in the meantime, having assembled a great host of their countrymen, suddenly rushed with noisy shouts on our men, who were laden with booty acquired by the most wicked means, and who were impeded by their sins, and put them to flight, wounding and slaying many as they retreated towards the ship; some of our people, choosing rather to trust to the mercy of the waves, and to perish by drowning, than to be slain at will by their enemies, threw themselves of their own accord into the waves, there to perish. Some of our knights they took alive, to imprison them; but, hearing that we had slain some of their nobles, and, above all, Naveth, son of Odo, a handsome and brave youth, they also hanged these knights of ours, after decapitating and mangling them dreadfully; finally, they tore their miserable corpses limb from limb, and threw them into the water, in detestation of their wicked greediness in not sparing the church, especially one belonging to religious men.

There fell in this conflict, on our side, some knights of the retinue of Richard, Earl of Cornwall, namely, Alan Bucel, Adam de Moia, Geoffrey Sturmy, and a fourth, Raymond, a Gascon crossbow-man, of whom the king used often to make sport; and about a hundred retainers were killed, besides those drowned, and the same number of the Welsh, or more. In the meantime, Sir Walter Bissett, who was aboard the ship with his followers, stoutly defended it, and was engaged till about midnight in continued fight with the Welsh, who fiercely attacked him on all sides, and our men, if they had not had the sides of the ship for a wall, would have altogether fallen into the hands of the enemy. At length, as the sea rose, the ship began to roll, and, it being now inaccessible, the Welsh withdrew, lamenting that our people had been snatched out of their hands. On board this ship were sixty casks of wine, besides other much-desired and seasonable provisions, of which we were at the time destitute. When morning came, and the tide receded, the Welsh returned with alacrity, thinking to seize on our people in the vessel, but, by God's providence, they had, during the night, when the tide was high, made their escape to us, by means of our boats, before the arrival of the Welsh, leaving only the ship. The Welsh, however, approached, carried off nearly all the wine and other things on board, and, leaving the ship as the tide rose, set fire to the vessel, a portion of which was consumed; the other part, however, was saved, in which were seven casks, which we dragged to the near shore.

Whilst we continued here with the army being in need of many things, we often sallied forth armed, and exposed ourselves to many great dangers, in order to procure necessaries, encountering many and various ambuscades and attacks from the Welsh, suffering much and often by the fortuitous chances of war, we also doing damage to them. After one conflict, we brought back in triumph to our camp the heads of nearly a hundred decapitated Welsh. At that time, there was such a scarcity of all provisions, and such want of all necessaries, that we incurred an irremediable loss both of men and horses. There was a time, indeed, when there was no wine in the king's house, and, indeed, not amongst the whole army, except one cask only; a measure of corn cost twenty shillings, a pasture ox three or four marks, and a hen was sold for eightpence. Men and horses consequently pined away, and numbers perished from want.'

Mathew Paris (c.1200-1259)
Chronica Masora

Castell y Bere

Sunlight, broken walls . . . cairns
in a field, washed by grass, patrolled
by sheep, cairns in a field. Heights
commanding the valley still. Oak
and hawthorn direct your feet, the path
circles, dips, ascends, a footbridge
jumps an abrupt chasm, you climb
to sunlight, broken walls . . .

Sunlight, broken walls . . . for six
centuries the Welsh carted them
off to build houses, barns, to separate
fields from fields. *Imagine then*
an Arthurian fortress perching upon the crag:
architecture pre-conquest,
towers D-shaped, circular, square,
curtain-walls four feet thick,

sanitation primitive. The well
contains water still. *Blood on the moss,*
blood on the stones. The English
picnic among the ruins, pleasured
by sunlight, broken walls . . .

Richard Poole

Glyndŵr

By the summer of 1404 Owain Glyndŵr had achieved the
fulfilment of Wales, and was recognized by most Welsh people as
their only prince. It was a moment roughly half-way through the
recorded history of the nation – six centuries since the making of
Offa's Dyke, six centuries before our own time – and Owain had
turned Wales into a State, presenting itself as of equal status
among the Powers of western Europe. Through its population was
small even by the standards of the time – perhaps 150,000 souls –
still it bore itself with some grandeur. It was like a fictional
kingdom of romance, out there on the fringe of Europe, sustaining
itself by force of arms, dependent upon ancient myth, upon vatic
declamations and suggestions of geomancy, to give it pride and
confidence. Like some barefoot magnifico out of the western
mountains, Owain Glyndŵr's princedom of Wales thrust itself
into the company of the nations.

At its head, indisputably, stood the hero. His image seems to
have been consciously arcane. If he had started life as a cultured
country gentleman of distinguished stock, he had become in his
middle years one of those self-recognized men of destiny who
appear now and then in the histories of all nations. Descended on
his father's side from princes of Powys in the north, on his
mother's from kings of Deheubarth in the south, he was
nevertheless a leader different in kind from the independent rulers
of the old Wales. He had no indigenous rivals, for one thing. The
Llywelyns had become rulers of all Wales by a process of long
calculation and conflict, but Owain's princedom was, so to speak,
his own invention: the old princely claims to sovereignty had long
since lapsed, and Owain was less a dynastic revivalist than a

91

political revolutionary. He claimed a throne that had never really existed, the throne of a Welsh State.

It was a visionary concept, and he achieved it by visionary means. Mystics and poets declared his divine calling. The whole teeming repertoire of Welsh fancy and folklore was summoned into the service of his cause. Prophecies of liberation were refurbished, newly interpreted or very possibly invented. Taliesin, the Old Man of Pencader, the birds of Llyn Safaddan, Owain Lawgoch, were conscripted as witnesses of providence. A web of fate was woven around the person of the prince, so that he acquired, among his subjects as among his enemies, a supernatural reputation: comets blazed at his birth, spirits obeyed him, the very elements were at his command.

He lived, in 1404, in the symbolic magnificence such a hero-figure needs. In the spring his soldiers had captured from the English the castle of Harlech, the most thrilling of all the fortresses Edward I had built to suppress the Welsh resistance. It stood in those days (for the geography has altered since) in a posture of supreme boldness on a high bluff immediately above the sea, and its four round towers could be seen in terrific silhouette from far along the Ardudwy coast, or stark against the mountainside across the water from Llŷn. To find Glyndŵr's ensign flying from the battlements of this prodigy must have been an inspiration in itself, but the meaning of his presence there was deeper still: for long before the English came to Wales at all, Harlech had been the seat of power of an earlier Welsh hero, Brân the Blessed himself.

Jan Morris
Wales: Epic Views of a Small Country (1998)

An Extraordinary Birth

OWEN GLENDOWER: . . . at my nativity
　　the front of heaven was full of fiery shapes,
　　of burning cressets: and at my birth
　　the frame and huge foundation of the earth
　　shaked like a coward.

HOTSPUR: Why, so it would have done at the same
　　season, if your mother's cat had but kitten'd,
　　though yourself had never been born.
OWEN GLENDOWER: I say the earth did shake when I was born.
HOTSPUR: And I say the earth was not of my mind,
　　If you suppose as fearing you it shook.
OWEN GLENDOWER: The heavens were all on fire, the
　　earth did tremble.
HOTSPUR: O, then the earth shook to see the heavens on fire,
　　and not in fear of your nativity.
　　Diseased nature oftentimes breaks forth
　　in strange eruptions; oft the teeming earth
　　is with a kind of colic pincht and vext
　　by the imprisoning of unruly wind
　　within her womb; which, for enlargement striving,
　　shakes the old beldam earth, and topples down
　　steeples and moss-grown towers. At your birth
　　our grandam earth, having this distemperature,
　　in passion shook.
OWEN GLENDOWER: Cousin, of many men
　　I do not bear these crossings. Give me leave
　　to tell you once again, that at my birth
　　the front of heaven was full of fiery shapes;
　　the goats ran from the mountains, and the herds
　　were strangely clamorous to the frighted fields.
　　These signs have marked me extraordinary,
　　and all the courses of my life do show
　　I am not in the roll of common men.
　　Where is he living, – clipt in with the sea
　　That chides the banks of England, Scotland, Wales, –
　　which calls me pupil, or hath read to me?
　　And bring him out that is but woman's son
　　can trace me in the tedious ways of art,
　　and hold me pace in deep experiments.

William Shakespeare (1564-1616)
from *King Henry IV*, Act III, Scene 1.

The Parliamentary Victory

The history of the campaigns of the Parliamentarians and the Royalists in Wales between 1642 and 1646 is complex and fragmentary; indeed it borders upon the incomprehensible when divorced from the pattern of fighting over the kingdom as a whole. After their crucial success in preventing the king from seizing London in October 1642, one of the aims of the leaders of the Parliamentary forces was to isolate Wales in order to prevent Charles from recruiting soldiers there, and to break the link between Ireland and the royal headquarters at Oxford. Control over the route from Pembroke through south Wales and on to Bristol and Oxford was therefore important to the strategy of the war. It changed hands several times between 1643 and 1645; by the winter of 1643, as a result of the efforts of Richard Vaughan of Golden Grove (the earl of Carbery), only Pembroke remained outside the control of the Royalists; the situation changed during the spring of 1644 when the Parliamentarians, under the leadership of Rowland Laugharne and with the support of the navy, captured all centres of importance in south Wales. From the summer of 1644 to the spring of 1645. Royalist control was reimposed by Charles Gerard, an able and ruthless soldier; Laugharne had some success against the Royalists in April 1645, but Gerard was again the master by early summer; by August, when Gerard was serving in England, Laugharne, with some assistance from disillusioned Royalists, had succeeded in recapturing almost the whole of south Wales; he was challenged by the Royalists during the winter of 1645-6, but following the fall of Raglan Castle in August 1646 all the counties of the south yielded to the Parliamentary forces.

John Davies
A History of Wales (1990)

Denbigh Castle: 1646

In 1646, we find the castle garrisoned by the loyalists: its governor was William Salusbury, of Bachymbyd, commonly called Salusbury Hosanau Gleision, or Blue Stockings. The siege was begun under the conduct of major general Mytton, about the 16th July; but such was the gallant defence of the besieged, that it was not surrendered till the 3rd of November, and then only on the most honourable conditions. It is very remarkable, that notwithstanding the orders of fallen majesty, in June, for the general surrender of every garrison in England and Wales, on fair and honourable terms, yet the first which yielded in North Wales, held out above two months longer than the last English castle.

Thomas Pennant (1726-1798)
Tours in Wales

Drowning a Witch

(Marion Eames' novel 'Y Stafell Ddirgel' (The Secret Room) is concerned with the persecution of Quakers in the Dolgellau area in the seventeenth century.

Early on in the book there is a vivid account of the drowning of a peasant woman who has been branded as a witch.)

Near the bridge, over the Wnion, there was a deep pool. Here scolds and witches were locked into the dreaded Red Chair and lowered into the water. If the woman managed to keep her head above water, this was proof that her soul had surely left her body for the devil was looking after his own. If she sank below the surface, she was innocent. But all too often proof came too late to save her life.

By the time the three men reached the green a large crowd had already gathered. Hywel pushed his way through with the aid of his sword and the people fell back to make way for the Squire of Hengwrt. The raucous voices and lewd laughter of the rabble deafened Rowland. By sunset beer and mead would have had their effect.

He almost stumbled over the wooden leg of an old soldier

whose drunken face leered into his own. A young woman tugged at his coat and screamed something unintelligible in his ear. She laughed hysterically as she let him go. Little boys from the town crept provocatively between the legs of the older people and no one heard their screams as they were trampled underfoot.

Suddenly, for an instant the crowd was silent – then, as if bidden by some unseen leader, the mob broke into loud cries: 'The witch. Here she is!' – 'To the Wnion with the witch!'

Yelling, they made way for a cluster of youths who were dragging an old woman behind them. Fear had made her staring eyes round as an owl's. Her wrinkled mouth, open wide in a scream, revealed one yellow fang of a tooth. Her grey hair hung in greasy knots over her shrunken shoulders. Desperately she tried to pull the remnants of her tattered clothing over the exposed flesh of her old body, and a hoot of laughter went up as one of the men tore her shirt apart to reveal her yellow, sagging breasts.

Rowland was sickened by the sight. He turned his head to look for Siôn Dafydd so that he could finish his business and escape.

At last he saw him – standing by the pool brandishing his whip. He was very drunk and bawling at the top of his voice.

'Come here, you – you skinny old crone. We'll see who's your master, by damn!'

He lashed the surface of the water wildly with his whip, wetting everyone within reach, while bystanders laughed and shouted their encouragement.

'Siôn Dafydd, the drover, for judge!'

'Forward the prisoner.'

'Come on, Siôn!' urged the men around him. 'Tell us if Betsan Prys is guilty or not.'

The old woman was thrust forward to stand shivering before the drover, who stared at her drunkenly, his flabby lips shining in his fat, red face.

'W-what is the charge?' he asked thickly, cracking his whip to another roar of laughter from the crowd.

A voice answered him: 'Bewitching the cows at Tynmynydd and making them dry.'

Other voices joined in: 'Dancing naked with the devil last Michaelmas!'

'She refused to go to church.'

'She poisoned Thomas Caerau's turnips.'

Siôn Dafydd raised his hand for silence.

'B-Betsan Prys,' he said, pointing his whip at the woman's face. 'You heard th-those ser-ious charges? What say you, hey?'

Betsan opened her mouth, but this time it was not to scream. Instead the crowd heard a softly-hissed, malevolent curse that struck terror in their hearts. There was no mistaking it. She had cursed Siôn Dafydd, the drover. The noisy laughter dwindled into uneasy silence. Siôn Dafydd fell back a step as if reeling from a blow. Some of the onlookers swiftly and secretly crossed themselves.

Gradually a murmur rose among them, spreading like a wind through the rushes. It became louder and louder like the approaching baying of blood-thirsty hounds. If previously some of them had felt compassion for Betsan Prys, they dared not show it now. She was doomed.

The young men heaved her up and held her high, a screaming, protesting bundle of rags. Then, not waiting to put her in the Red Chair, they flung her like a rat into the middle of the pool. The crowd, satisfied, pressed forward eagerly to watch her fate.

'She's sinking!'

A loud cry of disappointment greeted these words, but another cry quickly followed.

'No. No. There she is!'

'Once again!'

Rowland could stand it no longer. He tried to reach the end of the pool but was hemmed in on all sides by the surging crowd.

'Far better leave things as they are.' He turned to discover that the quiet voice beside him belonged to Dr Ellis, the Rector of Dolgellau. 'It's too late, in any case!'

Rowland knew the rector was right. How long, he wondered, did it take to drown a witch? He gazed with repugnance at the water where Betsan's face was appearing above the surface, her eyes closed, her mouth open.

He closed his own eyes and felt waves of nausea. He shivered. Dr Ellis was still talking in his thin, scholarly voice.

'A pity the Fair should end thus,' he said. 'But that's how it is.

None more cruel than an ignorant peasant full of fear.'
But what was there to fear in a poor old crone like Betsan? At first it had been little more than teasing. But when she had laid her curse on one of their company fear and hate had entered the game. Hatred always begat hatred.

Marion Eames
Y Stafell Ddirgel (The Secret Room) (1969)
Translated by the author

The Illusion
(The Greenfield Valley in Flintshire became one of the major industrial focal points in Wales in the eighteenth century. Thomas Pennant quotes the account of a factory owner concerning the accommodation provided for child apprentices. He does not question the accuracy of this.)

The cotton-twist company have between three and four hundred apprentices, which they clothe and feed themselves in commodious houses built for that purpose, the boys and girls in separate houses. These houses are white-washed every year, [and] are fumigated three times a week throughout every apartment, with smoke of tobacco . . . All the windows in the sleeping-rooms open at the tops, by which a thorough draft of air is admitted during the while time the children are at work. To these and other precautions the good state of health of so many children may be justly attributed; for though the number of apprentices have not been less than 300 for these seven years past, they have only buried seven. Their food for dinner is beef or pork and potatoes three or four times a week, the other days herrings and potatoes, or soup and bread and cheese, as much as they please to eat. Their breakfasts and suppers in summer is milk and bread; in the winter, when milk cannot be had, they drink porridge or broth, with bread and cheese. A surgeon is appointed to superintend their health; and a Sunday school is regularly attended by a master at each house.

Thomas Pennant (1726-1798)
A History of the Parish of Whitford

The Reality

(For an insight into the reality of conditions at the company we have to read these lines by John Jones, who was a child apprentice there. Not a great deal is known about him, but he was unusual in that he was living in a county which was considerably less anglicised than it is today, when most of those who wrote at all did so in Welsh.

The reference in the final line is to John Smalley, the owner of the company, who came from Preston.)

Well I remember, how in early years,
I toil'd therein, with unavailing tears . . .
No bondage state – no inquisition cell,
Nor scenes yet dearer to the Prince of Hell,
Could greater acts of cruelty display
Than yon tall factories on a former day;
E'en neighbouring forests frowned with angry nods,
To see, Oppression! thy demand for rods!
Rods doom'd to bruise in barbarb'rous dens of noise
The tender forms of orphan girls and boys!
Whose cries – which mercy in no instance foun'd,
Were in the din of whirling engines drown'd.
But all is past, and may Treffynnon see
No more of Foul Prestonian tyranny.

John Jones (1788-1858)
from *Holywell: A Poem*

Burying The Waste
(*Holywell*)

Trapped by Caradoc, favourite of a king,
even Winifred could not deny his sword.
Where hair leaked blood, a well of healing
sprang, then the stream hurrying its hoard
of news woke up the valley. Winifred
drew pilgrims limping, eager to be whole.
He signed up slaves of cotton, copper, lead.
Her stream, severed by water wheels, rolled
machines. When Winifred spread her arms wide

to make from shadows trees, he cut them down
but she thinned the Dee channel. Its quayside
became silent, the valley a ghost town.
Now buildings sprawl headless. All around,
sprung green, half-buried: still misshapen ground.

*   *   *

Not just the Church preferred its blessings high.
This cotton mill snatched six storeys of sky
with stone from the nearby abbey's shell
then, power untapped, St. Winifred's Well.
An act of God, a world in seventy days.
High too squire Pennant's recorded praise:
all the workers flourished, dined on meat,
fish 'in commodious houses'. Work was sweet.

Poet Jones of Llanasa, muffled voice
of the backwater – why couldn't he rejoice?
'Rods doom'd to bruise in barb'rous dens of noise
the tender forms of orphan girls and boys.'
Poets. They build nothing. Just hover, stare,
write maudlin history. Except he'd worked there.

*   *   *

Ingenuity flowers in such fumes.
New copper bolts were roots helping great ships
spread wide. Brass beakers moistening the lips
of Africa, exchanged for slaves, seemed blooms.

Up there, notice, a fly-wheel gouged the wall.
In this bank, too, an opening faced with brick
like an oven gone drowsily rustic;
no grass, webs or wormcasts though. Earth, that's all
almost. Hereabouts being where the knack

100

of refining human brushes took hold –
twigs bound in rags who carefully swept back
arsenic from this flue and lived to rot –
last year they found a skull, some ten-year-old
ingenuity planted then forgot.

*   *   *

The wall keeps on haemorraging dark green
through the bricked-up centuries, through soil
Meadow Mill injected with copper spoil.
And its damp spillway is coloured gangrene
in memory of times, as Pennant said,
when workers obeyed the 'antient law'
of sluicing thoroughly before meals or
watched 'eruptions of a green colour' spread.
(They knew dogs, if they licked the sheeting, slept
for good.) So justice as well, urbane,
copper-bottomed, is remembered here. Yet
through the wall's washed scrupulously by rain,
strange that metal still heaves through. Dogs drop.
It has tasted men and starves and cannot stop.

*   *   *

For three years, Frederick Rolfe alias
Baron Corvo, the Crow, pecked at the shell
of Holywell. He saw in it himself,
more idea than place, a proud man mostly
beak who squabbled, wrote and painted, furious
with 'Sewer's End', obscurity's rebel
till fury grew him wings. Two crows he left
in painted banners still caw 'Look at me!'

Flashing, art's narrowed gaze will open
on polluted water and turn even stones
to mirrors. The Well running wheels ran men.

Its stream's 'uproll and downcarol' Manley
Hopkins sang rang walls from where Poet Jones,
apprenticed to heartache, jumped to sea.

*　　*　　*

Ice tore a trench to the estuary.
Grass healed its sides. Water devised a well.
An idea, grown around it like a tree
surviving as an arched stone spell,
towered so pilgrims are still beckoned here,
a welling of belief that named a town.
When another idea for water
bricked up the flow, its weight wore people down.

The centuries keep waking to change dreams.
Dug from the undergrowth: brickwork's feud
with stone for possession of the stream.

And voices insisting water is alive –
those pursuing always and, pursued,
those in need of miracles to survive.

John Davies

(Editor's note: Frederick Rolf lived at Holywell from 1895 to 1898 where he
painted religious banners and became the editor of a local newspaper. He made
many enemies in the area. He dubbed himself 'Baron Corvo' and wrote fiction,
his best known novel being *Hadrian VII*. A.J.A. Symons wrote his biography, *The
Quest for Corvo* [1934].)

The Merthyr Rising

On that oppressively hot and thundery Friday morning, the
vanguard of the crowd, with its banner, pulled into Forman's Field
near the mansion of Penydarren House, to watch the eighty
Highlanders go by, led by William Crawshay, who had greeted

them at Cyfarthfa and by the magistrates Bruce and Hill, who had cut through side-streets to meet them at the Pandy by Tydfil's Well. According to one observer, the people were 'sullen and sturdy and kept the sides of the road under the walls, not choosing to be driven before the soldiers into town'.

In fact, with the banner and its cohorts looming behind, the detachment of the 93rd marched through lines of people who hissed and shouted 'Reform!'. Gangs of men and women and children paraded in front of them in mockery. 'Look at them! . . . See how few they are! . . . They're in our hands! . . . The game's ours!' Cries, insults, jeers in Welsh flew through the narrow streets at the uncomprehending heads of the soldiers. The crowd had come ready for trouble; hundreds of them carried makeshift weapons, clubs, bludgeons, mandrels, an iron bar, pit timber, hedge stakes, even the side of a wheelbarrow; the rearguard carried its ropes. And now, here they were, the men whose coming had been awaited with a tautening of the stomach and a quickening of the breath: uniforms, commands, a drilled impersonality, the muskets and the bayonets. They were face to face now with the naked power of the State, the ultimate sanction of sovereignty, the men with the licence to kill. But they were so few! A dangerous exhilaration, a giddy sense of irresponsible power recharged the tension of the stifling day.

The troops halted outside the Castle Inn, where the Specials were assembled, while the head of the crowd swept on down the road and hundreds massed around the banner directly outside the front door on its tier of steps rising from the pavement. More and more joined; people packed the doors and windows of the surrounding houses, crowded on the roofs. Observers inside the Castle estimated them at anything from 7,000 to 10,000. At the Castle were the bulk or the Trade of Merthyr, armed as special constables, the High Sheriff of Glamorgan, the magistrates of Merthyr and the communities around, three of the four ironmasters of the town. Outside were thousands of angry and excited demonstrators, ironstone miners, colliers, puddlers; women and shouting children, hundreds of the curious and the expectant. The hard core were the men of yesterday, massed around their Red Flag with its loaf of bread. Lewis Lewis was there, standing by William Williams and his banner; so were David Jones, *Dai Solomon*, and David Hughes. Others were singled out as scapegoats later: David Richards, a miner of 31 with whom 'the notorious Betsy Paul' had lived; Richard Lewis, *Dic Penderyn*, a miner of 23, who had thrashed the constable *Shoni Crydd* (John the Shoemaker) and had fought with Tories on the night of the illumination, a twenty-two year old puddler Thomas Richards, a cordwainer Joseph Prothero and two twenty-five year old labourers, Thomas Kinsey of Cefn and James Bird who had led the Reform raids in Dowlais. Of the ten men who were to answer to the law for their actions this day outside the Castle Inn, five were ironstone miners and two were puddlers.

So tense and urgent were the magistrates that they had the Riot Act read before the troops had been effectively deployed. Bread and cheese were brought out to the tired and sweating soldiers as the crowds pressed around them on all sides. Major Falls, their commander, asked the people to fall back. For a moment they did, but then pressed forward again, trying to talk the Highlanders into sedition, mocking them, shouting. The Specials were ordered to drive the crowd back. They ran into the wall of hatred that now divided Village and Inhabitants of the Ironworks and utterly failed. Bruce concentrated them in and around the passage of the Inn as the soldiers, by platoon, went into the Castle, took off their knapsacks and came out again with weapons at the ready. It was while this manoeuvre was in train, that Richard Hoare Jenkins, High Sheriff of Glamorgan, got up on a chair on the Inn steps and read the Riot Act. After he'd started, Bruce asked William Rowland the time; it was 10.40 by the bar clock. When Jenkins finished, Bruce followed in Welsh and took up his station by the door. The crowd replied with a great roar of defiance and raised a forest of clubs.

Gwyn A. Williams (1925-1995)
The Merthyr Rising

A Delayed Campaign

Lawyers have launched a campaign to gain a posthumous pardon for a working-class hero who was executed nearly 170 years ago.

Dic Penderyn – real name Richard Lewis – was hanged in 1831, at the age of 23, for his part in the Merthyr Tydfil uprising, when he wounded a soldier.

However, a lawyer believes that Penderyn, who led the revolt by mineworkers, was the victim of a miscarriage of justice, and has launched a bid for a posthumous pardon, claiming that he did not commit the crime.

Cardiff solicitor Bernard de Maid, who is currently fighting for an appeal for North Wales-born Ruth Ellis, the last woman to be hanged in Britain, has taken on the case at the request of descendants of Penderyn's family.

The 1831 riots, which saw a red flag being raised for the first time as crowds defied units of yeomanry and soldiers in a week of protest over low wages and poverty, created the first martyr of the Welsh working classes.

Western Mail, 2nd May, 2000

The Chartists at Newport

On 4 Nov. 1839 a large body of Chartists, many thousands in number, well armed, headed by the well-known Mr John Frost, late a magistrate of the place, marched into the town of Newport, co. Monmouth, from the hills, and commenced a violent attack on the Westgate Hotel, where the magistrates were sitting. After in vain remonstrating with the insurgents, the Riot Act was read, and the besieged, which fortunately included a party of the 42nd Foot, were compelled to fire upon the rioters, who fled in all directions, leaving behind them a great quantity of arms, ten or eleven men killed, and from thirty to forty wounded. Several of the special constables and soldiers were wounded, some of them severely. The Mayor, T. Phillips, Esq., was shot in the arm and hip. But for the firmness and promptitude of the authorities, the town of

Newport would have become a heap of smoking ruins.

In appears that, according to a preconcerted arrangement, on Saturday night (Nov. 2), the men began their march from the 'hills' in the neighbourhood of Merthyr, etc., armed with muskets, pikes, crowbars, pickaxes, etc., dividing into various columns, one to attack Newport, another to keep in check the soldiers stationed at Brecon, while a third marched towards Monmouth, to liberate Vincent, their former leader, from the gaol. After which they were unitedly to seize the whole of South Wales.

With these purposes their march was continued, the rioters sacking the villages in their route, seizing the provisions, and compelling the whole of the adult male population to join them. At all the iron-works, etc., they blew out the furnaces. At four o'clock on Monday morning they halted in Tredegar Park, the seat of Sir Charles Morgan, Bart., where they awaited for about two hours for the junction of another division from Pontypool and its neighbourhood.

The junction having been made, they formed at about six o'clock into two divisions, and marched into Newport, the one division marching down Stowhill, the other through Charles-street, and both joining in the centre of the main-street. On arriving at the Westgate Inn, they gave three cheers, and proceeded to attack the house, where they were so effectually checked. Frost and several others have been committed to Monmouth gaol, and a special commission will be issued for their trial.

On the 9th Nov. Lord Normanby addressed a letter to the Mayor of Newport, expressing Her Majesty's high approval of the conduct of the magistrates; and on the 13th Nov. his Lordship addressed another letter to the Mayor, Thomas Phillips, jun., Esq., (whose term of office has now expired), offering him, with Her Majesty's gracious sanction, the honour of Knighthood.

Anon, *Gentleman's Magazine* (1840)

Rebecca

Carmarthenshire was the focus of the Rebecca riots that broke out in 1843, and reached their height in 1844, against the turnpike gates. Roads throughout England had been very bad, and the network of magnificent highways cast over France by Napoleon put us to shame. The Government had accordingly improved, widened, and straightened the main roads, and the cost was to be defrayed by those who passed over them, by the means of turnpikes. Bodies of men assembled, disguised as women, with red cloaks, frilled caps, and peaked hats, their faces blackened, under the leadership of a tall man similarly disguised, who was entitled 'Rebecca', and his retinue, the daughters, from a strange misapplication of a passage in Genesis xxiv. 60: 'And they blessed Rebekah, and said unto her, Thou art our sister, be thou the mother of thousands of millions, and let thy seed possess the *gate* of those which hate them.'

Owing to the thinly populated state of the country, the attacks made by these bands on the toll-bars were successful, and for a while were carried on with impunity.

For some months a mob of about six hundred men, many of them mounted, were wont to assemble near St. Clear's, west of Carmarthen, and proceed to the destruction of toll-gates.

The turnpike would be ruthlessly cut to pieces, the house set on fire, and the occupants turned out, often in the depth of winter, to finish their night's rest in the open field, or to seek shelter in some solitary farm-shed on a mountain-top. Unfortunately the rioters proceeded to acts of personal violence, and an old woman, a gate-keeper at Hendy, was brutally murdered.

Not a syllable of information that availed was picked up by the magistrates. The whole of the population seemed to be sworn to secrecy. The contagion spread rapidly into Cardigan, Pembroke, and Glamorgan; nearly all South Wales was in a condition bordering on insurrection. Rewards were offered for information, the military were sent into the districts, but Rebecca kept her own counsel, and proceeded to more daring outrages. The military were harassed nightly by false alarms; Rebecca was like Will-o'-the-wisp, her followers spectral forms. At last a division of the

Metropolitan Police was sent to the aid of the soldiers. Matters became worse. The destruction of turnpikes was succeeded by attacks on dwelling-houses, by incendiarism, and threats of murder. A mob of many thousand persons on horse and foot entered Carmarthen in broad day, with the avowed 'intention of destroying the workhouse'. Had not a detachment of dragoons by forced marches reached the town in time, the mob would have effected its purpose.

A weir on the river Teifi, at Llechryd, a few miles above Cardigan, had long been a bone of contention between the fishermen and the owner. It precluded salmon, with which the river swarmed, from ascending, and so inflicted an injury on the country above. Rebecca in vain insisted on its removal. At four o'clock one morning about four hundred men, under the conduct of Rebecca, provided with crowbars, pickaxes, and other instruments, assembled at the weir; and in two hours had completely demolished the structure.

This strange outbreak at length began to die away. Two of the ringleaders, who were caught, made full confessions, and were sentenced to transportation. According to them, a leading magistrate of Llanelly was at the bottom of the whole movement.

Sabine Baring Gould (1834-1924)
A Book of South Wales

A Vision of Hell

(*In Borrow's immortal 'Wild Wales' the author includes a vivid impression of the effect of industrialisation on the Wrexham area in the mid nineteenth century.*)

I soon reached Rhiwabon. There was a prodigious noise in the public-houses as I passed through it. 'Colliers carousing,' said I. 'Well, I shall not go amongst them to preach temperance, though perhaps in strict duty I ought.' At the end of the town, instead of taking the road on the left side of the church, I took that on the right. It was not till I had proceeded nearly a mile that I began to be apprehensive that I had mistaken the way. Hearing some people coming towards me on the road I waited till they came up:

they proved to be a man and a woman. On my inquiring whether I was right for Llangollen the former told me that I was not, and in order to get there it was necessary that I should return to Rhiwabon. I instantly turned round. About half-way back I met a man who asked me in English where I was hurrying to. I said to Rhiwabon, in order to get to Llangollen. 'Well, then,' said he, 'you need not return to Rhiwabon – yonder is a short cut across the fields,' and he pointed to a gate. I thanked him and said I would go by it; before leaving him I asked to what place the road led which I had been following.

'To Pentré Castren,' he replied. I struck across the fields and should probably have tumbled half a dozen times over pales and the like, but for the light of the Cefn furnaces before me which cast their red glow upon my path. I debouched upon the Llangollen road near to the tramway leading to the collieries. Two enormous sheets of flame shot up high into the air from ovens, illumining two spectral chimneys as high as steeples, also smoky buildings, and grimy figures moving about. There was a clanging of engines, a noise of shovels and a falling of coals truly horrible. The glare was so great that I could distinctly see the minutest lines upon my hand. Advancing along the tramway I obtained a nearer view of the hellish buildings, the chimneys and the demoniac figures. It was just such a scene as one of those described by Ellis Wynn in his Vision of Hell. Feeling my eyes scorching I turned away, and proceeded towards Llangollen, sometimes on the muddy road, sometimes on the dangerous causeway. For three miles at least I met nobody. Near Llangollen, as I was walking on the causeway, three men came swiftly towards me. I kept to the hedge, which was my right; the two first brushed roughly past me, the third came full upon me and was tumbled in to the road. There was a laugh from the two first and a loud curse from the last as he sprawled in the mire. I merely said 'Nos Da'ki,' and passed on, and in about a quarter of an hour reached home, where I found my wife awaiting me alone, Henrietta having gone to bed being slightly indisposed. My wife received me with a cheerful smile.

George Borrow (1803-1881)
Wild Wales

The Launch of the 'Royal Charter'

(The sinking of the 'Royal Charter' off the northern coast of Anglesey in 1859 is generally regarded as one of the greatest maritime disasters of all time. She was returning with goods and passengers from Australia when she ran into a very severe storm not very far from Moelfre. The captain gradually lost control of his ship and it met a tragic end on what is, at the best of times, a precarious part of the Welsh coastline. Out of an estimated 498 people on board only 40 survived, and some of these were crew members. A month or so after the tragedy Charles Dickens visited Moelfre and talked to local people about it and the resulting journalistic item eventually appeared in his book 'The Uncommercial Traveller'. But, interestingly, a major American novelist, Nathaniel Hawthorne, had been present when 'The Royal Charter' had been launched on the Dee at Sandycroft in Flintshire, where she was built at the iron works. Things did not go according to plan then and some saw this as an omen of what was to follow.)

August 2nd, 1855

Mr – has urged me very much to go with his father and family to see the launch of a great ship which has been built for their house, and afterwards to partake of a picnic; so, on Tuesday morning I presented myself at the landing-stage, and met the party, to take passage for Chester. It was a showery morning, and looked woefully like a rainy day; but nothing better is to be expected in England; and, after all, there is seldom such a day that you cannot glide about pretty securely between the drops of rain. This, however, did not turn out one of those tolerable days, but grew darker and darker, and worse and worse; and was worst of all when we had passed about six miles beyond Chester, and were just on the borders of Wales, on the hither side of the river Dee, where the ship was to be launched. Here the train stopped, and absolutely deposited our whole party of excursionists, under a heavy shower, in the midst of a muddy potato-field, whence we were to wade through mud and mire to the ship-yard, almost half a mile off. Some kind Christian, I know not whom, gave me half of his umbrella, and half of his cloak, and thereby I got to a shed near the ship, without being entirely soaked through.

The ship had been built on the banks of the Dee, at a spot where it is too narrow for her to be launched directly across, and so she lay lengthwise of the river, and was so arranged as to take water parallel with the stream. She is, for aught I know, the largest ship in the world; at any rate, longer than the *Great Britain*, – an iron-screw steamer, – and looked immense and magnificent, and was gorgeously dressed out in flags. Had it been a pleasant day, all Chester and half Wales would have been there to see the launch; and, in spite of the rain, there were a good many people on the opposite shore, as well as on our side; and one or two booths, and many of the characteristics of a fair, – that is to say, men and women getting intoxicated without any great noise and confusion.

The ship was expected to go off about twelve o'clock, and at that juncture all Mr –'s friends assembled under the bows of the ship, where we were little sheltered from the rain by the projection of that part of the vessel over our heads. The bottle of port wine with which she was to be christened was suspended from the bows to the platform where we stood by a blue ribbon; and the ceremony was to be performed by Mrs – , who, I could see, was very nervous in anticipation of the ceremony. Mr – kept giving her instructions in a whisper, and showing her how to throw the bottle, and as the critical moment approached, he took hold of it along with her. All this time we were waiting in momentary expectation of the ship going off, everything being ready, and only the touch of a spring, as it were, needed to make her slide into the water. But the chief manager kept delaying a little longer, and a little longer; though the pilot on board sent to tell him that it was time she was off. 'Yes, yes; but I want as much water as I can get,' answered the manager; and so he held on till, I suppose, the tide had raised the river Dee to its very acme of height. At last the word was given; the ship began slowly to move; Mrs – threw the bottle against the bow with a spasmodic effort that dashed it into a thousand pieces, and diffused the fragrance of the old port all around, where it lingered several minutes. I did not think that there could have been such a breathless moment in an affair of this kind.

The ship moved majestically down toward the river; and unless it were Niagara, I never saw anything grander and more impressive than the motion of this mighty mass as she departed from us. We on the platform, and everybody along both shores of the Dee, took off our hats in the rain, waved handkerchiefs, cheered, shouted, – 'Beautiful!' 'What a noble launch!' 'Never was so fair a sight!' – and, really, it was so grand, that calm, majestic movement, that I felt the tears come into my eyes. The wooden pathway down which she was gliding began to smoke with the friction; when all at once, when we expected to see her plunge into the Dee, she came to a full stop. Mr – , the father of my friend, a gentleman with white hair, a dark, expressive face, bright eyes, and an Oriental cast of features, immediately took the alarm. A moment before his countenance had been kindled with triumph; but now he turned pale as death, and seemed to grow ten years older while I was looking at him. Well he might, for his noble ship was stuck fast in the mud of the Dee, and without deepening the bed of the river, I do not see how her vast iron hulk is ever to be got out.

Nathaniel Hawthorne (1804-1864)
from *Passages from the English Notebooks*

The Wreck

Only two short months had gone, since a man, living on the nearest hill-top overlooking the sea, being blown out of bed at about daybreak by the wind that had begun to strip his roof off, and getting upon a ladder with his nearest neighbour to construct some temporary device for keeping his house over his head, saw from the ladder's elevation as he looked down by chance towards the shore, some dark troubled object close in with the land. And he and the other, descending to the beach, and finding the sea mercilessly beating over a great broken ship, had clambered up the stony ways, like staircases without stairs, on which the wild village hangs in little clusters, as fruit hangs on boughs, and had given the alarm. And so, over the hill-slopes, and past the waterfall, and down the gullies where the land drains off into the ocean, the scattered quarrymen and fishermen inhabiting that part of Wales had come running to the dismal sight – their clergyman among them. And as they stood in the leaden morning, stricken with pity, leaning hard against the wind, their breath and vision often failing as the sleet and spray rushed at them from the ever forming and dissolving mountains of sea, and as the wool which was a part of the vessel's cargo blew in with the salt foam and remained upon the land when the foam melted, they saw the ship's life-boat put off from one of the heaps of wreck, and first, there were three men in her, and in a moment she capsized, and there were but two; and again, she was struck by a vast mass of water, and there was but one; and again, she was thrown bottom upward, and that one, with his arm struck through the broken planks and waving as if for the help that could never reach him, went down into the deep.

Charles Dickens (1812-1870)
The Uncommercial Traveller

Awakening

(Edward Tegla Davies' novel 'Gŵr Pen y Bryn' [The Master of Pen y Bryn] is set in North East Wales during the period of the tithe disturbances.)

The children had long been asking each other – and Hugh – who this 'tithe' was that everybody was talking about. They already had some glimmer, but these exciting occurrences called for a clear, definite view of the matter. Hugh did not know the tithe, and everyone was surprised, because Hugh knew everybody within miles of Llangeunant. Lewis thought he was the parson's brother. It was in the light of this revelation that he had a fight with Teddy, from Y Nant. When the carriage arrived, and everyone got excited, he decided it was the fellow with the rings and gold chain and the light-coloured hat. And since this kind of garb was unusual in Llangeunant, they decided that the tithe, however much people ran him down, was an extraordinary man. When the carriage had gone and the people had calmed down a bit, James the Crown's labourer, came up the steps to the barn. Everyone had to pass the Crown to get to Pen y Bryn, and everyone who was anyone stopped there for a drink, so they regarded James as the last word on all these topics. They made Lewis ask him whether the multicoloured gentleman in the carriage was, in fact, the tithe. James replied that the tithe was not a man but a place. But they could not understand why, if it was a place, you had to pay it, and why it was not mentioned in the geography book. In the middle of their arguments and discussions William Jones, Y Graig, came by. He was one of the eager crowd surrounding the Crown, and there was a rumour that the next auction would be at his home. Lewis asked him if he could please tell them where the tithe was. William Jones stopped short, and looked Lewis straight in the eye till he blushed to the roots of his hair. He went on looking at him till he shuffled his feet backwards and forwards and on top of each other, and finally tugged at his coat buttons and chewed his nails, his lips trembling. Lewis saw from William Jones' face that asking a sensible man about the tithe was something more awful than he had ever dreamed of.

'Well,' said William Jones at last, slowly, 'since you are so incredibly stupid, I must enlighten you, for the future good of Wales. The tithe is not a geographical location but a principle.' Whereupon he took himself off. After this the children all remained quite still and mute for a long while, looking at each other, and thinking, and Hugh, who was with them, tried to follow suit. They realised that the world they were in was stranger than they imagined, and they threw furtive, uneasy glances towards the school, secretly suspecting that this, after all, was the safest place. They had never heard of principle, as far as they knew, it might well be something terrible, judging by William Jones' expression when he talked about it, and since it had to do with Wales of the Future. Hugh slunk away from them, and made for Pen y Bryn across the fields; Jimmy began to cry. Then they heard a heavy carriage, and the people – they were a crowd by now – stirred and moved excitedly around. The lads craned their necks and saw the manes of two horses coming into view past the crossroads, followed by a brake full of policemen. Some of the bystanders shouted welcome, but a hail of mud fell on them which considerably dampened their enthusiasm. The brake of policemen went by, ignoring everybody, and the shuffling and weaving started up again, the boys clinging tightly to each other.

Soon a cloud of dust was seen rising over a hillock from the Coedarglodd Road, and a tramp, tramp, tramp sound approaching: someone shouted 'Halt', and there was a great silence. Many faces grew pale, and many hearts palpitated, and yet no one wanted to run away. The boys squeezed up against the barn door as far as they could, and Lewis made sure the door was unlocked. Someone shouted over the hillock: 'Quick march,' and the steady, continuous, tramp, tramp, tramp started up again. About 200 miners from the lime quarries of Craig y Mwyn came into view, as orderly as an army of soldiers; each one had a spade, a crowbar, or pickaxe, or sledge-hammer across his shoulder, like a gun. Every worker bearing a farm implement, whom they had picked up on their four-mile journey from Craig y Mwyn to the Crown, was with them. The look on their faces haunted everyone that saw them, for the rest of their lives. Their faces had that look – seen about once or twice in a lifetime – of the soul of a people awakening.

E Tegla Davies (1880-1967)
Gŵr Pen y Bryn (The Master of Pen y Bryn)
Translated by Nina Watkins

A Superb Orator

'*Anyone who has lived in these mountain regions knows what sickness means there. There are miles of track, broken and rutted by the winter rains, before you even reach the high road. The people there never send for medical aid for petty ailments. The doctor is not even summoned for important family events. He is only called in when life is in jeopardy. Here in this district you have fifty square miles without a doctor. Ask anybody who has lived on a wayside farm in these districts or in the villages in the valleys, and they will tell you that one of the most vivid memories of their youth was to be wakened up in the dead of night by hearing the clatter of a horse ridden furiously past in the dark, and everyone knew there was a dire struggle for life going on in the hills.*'

David Lloyd George was a superb orator in both Welsh and English. He was also one of the few who could command both the House of Commons and the public platform where a different technique was necessary. In a full House, there would be 650 members packed into a small chamber; on the hustings in the late nineteenth and early twentieth centuries there would be thousands listening to him in vast Halls or in the open air. Unfortunately, we do not have recordings of his most famous speeches since the recording industry was in its infancy when his oratorical powers were at their greatest. However, the quotation, from a speech in the House of Commons in 1912, gives an idea of his immense spell-binding skill. Add to the carefully constructed sentences, his tenor voice with its remarkable carrying power, his brilliant blue eyes, ('I first fell in love with his eyes' – Frances Stevenson), and dramatic gestures, we understand why he is ranked with the greatest orators in British history.

Rufus Adams
David Lloyd George: The Formative Years 1863-1890,
the text of a lecture delivered in 1994.

The 'Titanic' : A Welsh Connection

(Dai Bowen, the lightweight boxing champion, was one of the 1,513 passengers who lost their lives when this ship sank on April 15th, 1912. On April 12th the ship had stopped at Cherbourg in France. From here Dai wrote a letter home to his mother in Treherbert.)

My Dear Mother,
I am just writing you a few lines before I go sick for I have been very good so far. This is a lovely boat, she is very near so big as Treherbert, she is like a floating palace, against you walk from one end of her to the other you are tired. We are landing in France the time I am writing you this, you don't know whether she is moving or not she goes very steady. Dear Mother, I hope that you won't worry yourself about me, I can tell you I am a lot better than I thought I would be, for we gets plenty of fun on board. We met two Swansea boys at the station, so you see that I get plenty of company. There is hundreds of foreigners on her of every nation. The food we get here is very good but not so good as dear old home. We have no boxing gloves with us, they would be no good if we did have some. Remember me to Martha Jane & Jack & Tommy Ostler, tell Morris & Stephen that if I will feel like I do now when I land in Yankee Land I shall be alright. I shan't give you no address now, not until I land for it won't be worth. I did

116

not see David Rees in Southampton at all. Remember me to all I know, tell Stephen to tell all the boys that I am enjoying myself alright so far.

If James tell you that I have not wrote to him, tell him that I can't do it very good now, you can show him this if you like, for it will be the same I shall have to say now for the time being as I am telling you.

I hope you will excuse the pencil for I have no pen and ink, so cheer up now mother, for I am in the pink, so don't vex. I think I will draw to a close now in wishing you all my best love.

From you loving son, David John.

In the Trenches

(R.G. Evans, who was born in Leeswood in Flintshire, has left a diary in which he writes of his experiences as a quartermaster during the First World War. He conveys vivid impressions of the horror and carnage of life in the trenches at that time. The document is deposited at the Flintshire Archives Department at Hawarden.)

10th June 1916: We left at 3–0 pm and marched to the trenches. We arrived at the firing line' the same day at about 7–0 pm for our first dose. We were attached to the 2nd RMF for instruction.

The people, who live in the area are mostly coalminers. The mines are very up to date, each one having hot and cold shower baths for the workmen's use. We had a bath at one or two places and in one colliery I noticed a little electric car which hauled the coal in place of men or horses . . .

To the trenches as usual and found that Jenkins was slightly wounded, and just as I was leaving the line S and B came carrying a body and they told me that it was Edge who had been killed. I cannot say how sorry I am to hear this. He was badly knocked about and I shall never forget the words he spoke to Rattler as he was going into the line a few hours before death. Also I shall never forget my birthday. It was also in Jinks's dugout when I remembered it was July 6th and I was 21. The bosches were playing the deuce with us at the time and sending a lot of stuff over.

July 16th: Still quite well. Have managed to get through every night safely. I found out that the stench is caused by a horse which was blown up and nearly eaten away by rats. A shell must have dropped where he was buried.

Not far from Maroc on the way to Loos, where the great battle was fought, may be seen the graveyards of many French soldiers who have fallen. The French bury them where they fall. It is a sad sight to see the church at Bully Granary-tombs and graves blown up and the entire body of the church is blown away; the tower is also pretty groggy. I saw a large crucifix on the road. Some of the trees around it are damaged. The French attach an especial value to the crucifix.

October 6th: I had the shock of my life. Reg my brother, came to look for me. He was on horseback and had ridden from Bethune. He looked fine and I was delighted to see him.

Went to the trenches again. I got back safely, although I had many narrow squeaks. Machine guns were very busy and I was expecting a hit all the while but we all got through all right.

During this time in the line BC acted splendidly, and five men were recommended and one officer.

R.G. Evans (1895-1974)
in his unpublished diary

Glynmawr

In the spring of 1926, in Glynmawr, the green of the meadows was fresh and cool, and the blossom was white in the orchards, and on the thorns and crabs in the hedges. Along the banks of the roads the violets were hidden in overgrowing leaves, but the primroses were out, though not so thickly as on the banks of the railway, where they flowered most richly, as if the cuttings and embankments had been made for them. All over the valley, and far up on the mountains, innumerable birds sang and flew. The Honddu was high, as it had been since midwinter. The low-lying cottages near the river had already been flooded.

Here was the ordinary history of the valley, sheltered and almost isolated under its dark mountains. But now, with this May

Day, a different history exerted its pressures, and reached, with the railway line, even this far. The troubled years of strike and lock-out, which had affected the village only slightly, moved now to their crisis, and touched this valley under its lonely mountains. As April ended, the Government's subsidy to the coal industry ended with it. The miners refused the owners' new terms, and lock-out notices were already posted at the pits. Up beyond the mountains, little more than ten miles from this farming valley, lay the different valleys, where the pits and the colliers' houses were crowded. At dusk, above Darren, the glow of the steel furnace spread up each evening into the sky, and many turned now to watch it more seriously, and to think of the black valleys that lay hidden beyond. There was the trouble, that the eye could almost see, and in the papers the trouble was recorded, to be read in the sun of mid-morning among flowers and blossoming trees.

Raymond Williams (1921-1988)
Border Country

Point of Ayr

(Point of Ayr colliery, near Prestatyn, closed in 1996, after over a hundred years of coal production. The following previously unpublished item is extracted from an account of life in the pit, and the complete document will be found at the Flintshire Archives Office at Hawarden.)

Having been working underground at Point of Ayr colliery for forty six years you can imagine the changes I have seen taking place. I find that I started working at the colliery on June 18th 1930 at the age of seventeen, having previously worked at Prestatyn. How thrilled I was at the prospect of at least double the wage I had at Prestatyn i.e. ten shillings per week.

Having arrived at the colliery on my first day I was sent down to Pit Bottom. I found the only light available was an oil lamp you carried. My job was driving a pony called Norman. After being employed a fortnight I discovered that the annual trip was to take place, the venue being Southport. I was told I would be invited to go, but as I had only been employed a few months would not be given the pocket money of ten shillings which the others received.

One thing strikes me very forcibly and it is the fact that out of five hundred men employed at the time only one was an Englishman. How cosmopolitan the pit has become since those days! The banksman was an old hand, Joe Luke from Mostyn. Should he be absent his place would be taken by another old gentleman, William Jones, Y Mwynt, as he was known. He walked from Trelogan with his umbrella, starting out at 5–0 am. It was known for some of these old miners who walked from Trelogan, Newmarket, Penyffordd and Ffynongroew to turn back if they were only half way to the colliery when the starting hooter went – they would consider it too late to proceed! It was an understood thing that to arrive in the lamproom after 5–55 am meant no lamp for you, so it was home James!

Each man took an interest in the output obtained. The under manager, a cunning old gentleman, would come down the pit and tell the pit bottom lads that the surface men were waiting on them and at the same time he would phone the surface men informing them that pit bottom were waiting on them, with the result that he had created a competition between both sections. Work was commenced on drilling for a new seam and the dirt resulting from this drilling was wound up the pit on the night shift. The bankman was John Hugh Cooper, another elderly man. On one occasion when winding the dirt he forgot to release what is called the keps from under the stationary cage on the surface with the result that one cage was stationary and the other ascending. On seeing the slack rope he realised what he had failed to do but in his fright released the keps with the result that the cage dropped a hundred feet down the shaft. Fortunately the rope held, but the spindle on the headgear bent. Two days output was lost while the damage was repaired. The bankman was very upset over the incident and became ill, loosing time off work. After many months his worry became more intense and he decided to end it all by committing suicide.

Another accident I recall, a fireman, Robert Jones (Bob Newmarket) was injured badly. It seems that he was about his duty firing the coal, and evidently was using a shorter length of cable than was needed, with the result that when he fired he was

120

struck by a piece of coal which became embedded in his thigh. He was taken to hospital, but died within a few days.

. . . In 1934, a year that miners of my time will remember all their lives, the officials at Point of Ayr arranged a trip to Blackpool. This was to take place on a Saturday, the date September 24th. The trip party proceeded, as arranged, but for some reason was held up. Among the party were a number of the members of the colliery rescue team. On the Saturday morning news was received that a disaster had taken place at Gresford Colliery in the early hours of Saturday morning. A call for assistance from the Point of Ayr rescue team was sent along to Blackpool, but the party were still held up. When they did arrive in Blackpool they found it was time to return home, so they didn't see the illuminations. They proceeded to Wrexham. 239 lives were lost in the disaster, the second largest mining disaster in this country, the largest having taken place at Senghenydd in South Wales when 439 lives were lost.

R.G. Hughes
in his unpublished diary.

Sudden Perils

In other trades there are a thousand diversions to break the monotony of work – the passing traffic, the morning newspaper, above all, the sky, the sunshine, the wind and the rain. The miner has none of these. Every day for eight hours he dies, gives up a slice of his life, literally drops out of life and buries himself . . . Down below are the sudden perils – runaway trams hurling down the lines; frightened ponies kicking and mauling in the dark, explosions, fire, drowning. And if he escapes? There is a tiredness which . . . leads to stupor, which remains with you on getting up, and which forms a dull, persistent background to your consciousness.

From a speech by Aneurin Bevan quoted
in *The Daily Express* (1932)

War Clouds

There is an aeroplane up in the sky. You know the war is coming. The bicycle shed at school has already been sandbagged up so that we can all run there when Goering and Hitler have decided at a secret meeting that the time has come for *Scholae Crustensis* to go. Your Physics master tells you that it is a Whitley heavy bomber (actually quite light and helpless and used in war only to pull drogues for target practice) and you are aware suddenly of belonging to history. You are going to be part of this. The Physics master doesn't seem at all afraid. You hope that if you are still at school when the Heinkels come you are having physics lessons although you hate them; the Phys. Lab. is next to the bicycle shed.

The war goes on. So does the process of education. You find languages easy, and your first published work is an English poem in the school magazine. It is an epic and starts:

At Chemistry he was a stue,
All the elements he knew,
But he learned about war gasses
At the town's A.R.P. classes . . .

T. Glynne Davies (1926-1976)
in an essay, in *Artists in Wales*
edited by Meic Stephens

On the Home Front

25 September 1944
It's no good. We're too used to a black-out. Having no curtains at all on the scullery and bathroom windows made us feel too guilty, naked and unprotected, so I've had to put some back. Mama, knowing that there was a light showing outside while I was at choir practice last night was too frightened of being alone.

I came home as pleased as Punch today because I'd got a ½ packet of gingerbread biscuits. They're quite good too, so we had them instead of pudding. Did we enjoy them! I had to give four points out of a precious twenty but it was well worth it. We managed to save twenty last month (out of forty made up of twenty each) so we can have a 1 lb. tin of salmon. It is difficult for anybody living alone, because then they can really never afford a tin of salmon without sacrificing everything else. It's a pity there aren't any ½ lb. tins available.

Edna Gwynne Davies in her diary
deposited in the Denbighshire Archives Department

A Wartime Escapade
(During the turbulent years between 1939 and 1945 some unexpected incidents occurred in Wales. The following story appeared in the 'Sunday Express'.)

3 Boys and a Platoon of Marines

With three rifles and 400 rounds of 0.22 ammunition, three boys aged 12 to 14 defied a platoon of marines 36 strong, led by two subalterns, in the Welsh mountains round Cader Idris. For two days and nights they carried out their own guerrilla warfare, only surrendering under the protection of a white flag when reduced to two rounds of ammunition.

On Thursday the boys broke into the armoury of a camp at Barmouth. Three rifles and all the ammunition were taken. Soon the theft was discovered and a hue and cry started. The lieutenant-quarter-master was recalled from leave, and the brigadier's batman sent after the young desperadoes.

When bullets started whizzing round his head, he decided that reinforcements were needed and went back for the regimental police.

They in turn retired in the face of superior enemy fire and the National Fire Service were called out. They gave up. The boys were all night on the mountain and shot two fowls belonging to a local poultry-keeper. They then went to a disused mine in the mountains and dug themselves in.

On Friday, a platoon of marines, 36 strong with two subalterns, set out on the chase. They tracked the boys down and the bullets began flying again. The platoon got under cover and prepared to attack. Firing blank cartridges, they made a frontal assault on the boys' position, but had to retreat. Reinforcements were sent for, and a captain came to supervise.

Ammunition was running low and the boys flew a white flag. Out they came, with just two rounds, but without the rifles, which have not been found yet. The three were marched back to their home town, under an escort of eight marines. The boys were placed 'under restriction' at their homes, but last night went to the local cinema, feted by all the boys.

Sunday Express, February 20th 1944

Tryweryn

'Nothing's gone that matters – a dozen farms,
A hollow of no great beauty, scabby sheep,
A gloomy Bethel and a field where sleep
A few dead peasants. There are finer charms
Observed in rising water, as its arms
Circle and meet above the walls; in cheap
Power and growing profits. Who could reap
Harvests as rich as this in ploughmen's palms?
All's for the best – rehoused, these natives, too,
Should bless us for sanitation and good health.
Later, from English cities, see the view
Misty with hiraeth – and their new-built wealth.'

'All of our wealth's in men – and their life's blood
Drawn from the land this water drowns in mud.'

Sally Roberts Jones

A Village That Drowned

My mother once told me of a village that drowned. 'The people were all right' she said quickly; I was small then, and it was important to me that people be all right. 'They moved away.'

'Where did they go?'

'Scattered far and wide.'

She looked towards the window as if they would be out there, walking down the street with their suitcases. It sounded like a story but she said it was true.

'Did the people want to go?'

'No they didn't want to go.'

'Why did they, then?'

'They had to. The valley was needed for a reservoir. A big lake,' she explained, 'To keep water in for people to use.'

'The people of the village?'

'No, English people,' and she frowned.

'But what happened to the houses?'

'The houses are still there under the water.'

I tried to imagine it; a house like my nan's, with the china dogs still fierce on the mantelpiece, and seaweed curtains waving in the green water. Tea cosies like jelly fish, rugs like rays swimming over coral sofas. There would be no point in closing the doors; you could just float out of the window and look down on the map of your garden, at the whole village under water like a present from the seaside. Tryweryn. Cwm Atlantis. A tap turns in Liverpool, and a church steeple breaks the surface of a Welsh lake.

Siân Preece
——from 'Running Out', included in
From the Life and Other Stories (2000)

Aberfan

The word is written across the top of my mind
In thick black letters.
It has become public property.

When the black piper called the tune
And smothered those young faces
Sitting in the beginning of the day,
Orderly in their desks, then
After the frantic and hopeless clawing
Of the elders at the murderous slurry, now
All we have is a name,
Clawlike and terrible, in black.

There was of course no time for panic –
They were snuffed out in split seconds
As efficiently as in a nuclear blast.

The Queen visited the scene.
The cold funeral with its cross of wreaths
Laid out across the floor of the valley
Came to us by courtesy of film and television.

The magazines received a flood of verse to mark the spot.
The customary fund for relatives was set up
And money poured in.
Toys piled up in the railway station.
Perhaps the grieving parents can forgive such mockeries.

That Friday I was in London.
We went to a bookshop on Charing Cross Road
Where in the dark lower rooms
Three Welshmen stood by the wireless
Listening to the news from Wales.
They had known all this before.
Their shelves were full of memorials.

Later, driving to work,
The flags were at half-mast,
And I thought,
That is fitting.

Few things are fitting
Except silence.

                                                    John Idris Jones

A Wise and Trusted Leader

The Revd. Hayes had been inducted to the Baptist pastorate at Merthyr Vale a year or so before the disaster struck at Aber-fan. His manse was in Moy Road, not a hundred yards away from Pant-glas Junior School where his two sons, Dyfrig, aged nine and Gwilym, aged seven, were pupils. On the morning of Friday 21 October 1966 he heard the roar of what he thought was a jet crashing into the side of Merthyr Mountain above the village. The sound, in fact, was that of No. 7 tip ripping the junior school apart with the loss of over 120 lives. One of the first to arrive on the scene, he assisted with the rescue for many hours knowing that his eldest son was somewhere in the wreckage. Finding that he could help no more he then began a sorrowful pastoral round comforting the bereaved. It was 11 p.m. before he joined the queue outside the makeshift mortuary in Bethania chapel to see whether the body of Dyfrig had been brought in. His pastoral round continued throughout the next day, and although the inevitable news of his son's death was broken to him during that evening, he was in his pulpit as usual on Sunday morning. After having read from scripture he made a plea for an end to the tipping of coal waste throughout the valleys, then he said:

Let us thank God that things are not worse. We must not be bitter but must approach it with a spirit of love. Let us be thankful for miracles and thank God for those who survived.

When the congregation sang 'Safe in the arms of Jesus', he broke down and wept.

Like the senseless slaughter of the Somme and the Holocaust for the Jews, the Aber-fan disaster called into question virtually all the truths of people's conventional understanding of the divine: God's involvement in creation, his providential ordering of the world and above all the suffering of the innocent. The problem of theodicy was made even more emotive by its context in the historical development of south Wales. Coal, which had been the mainstay of the Welsh industrial economy for nearly a century, capitalism and human rapaciousness as well as questions of faith and meaning were all seen to have a bearing on the calamity. Yet if the cry of dereliction was heard on that misty autumn morning, in the midst of tragedy there was evidence too of the divine pity and, haltingly but unmistakably, the hope of resurrection as well. 'Two or three people did ask me in the first days, "Why did God allow this tragedy to happen?" but I have not heard it since then,' the Revd Hayes recalled. 'From my correspondence I would say that this question has been asked much more by people outside Aber-fan'. In the years following Kenneth Hayes was to become one of the community's wisest and most trusted leaders, ensuring that Christianity had yet its part to play in even a secular Wales.

D. Densil Morgan
from the *New Welsh Review* (1998)

A load of coal

(in memory of my grandfather killed in the mines, and in tribute to the miners on strike, 1984-5)

A storm of hail
used to come to the gable end,
regular too, in season –
rough lumps of it
bright and clean.

The overseer there was Gran,
counting in more than a load
of 'compo' coal,
remembering that fireless morning
when the news came –
              an accident
below ground
              and Grandad in it.

The fire of life's so fierce,
so cold its embers –
the invisible scorch to the heart.

To us, grief means cheap coal.

After everyone else had left
she went to her solitary Aberfan,
to the shed, to fondle and reproach
hard coal that's never quenched.

Menna Elfyn
Translated by the poet

Elegy for the Welsh Dead, in the Falkland Islands, 1982

Gŵyr a aeth Gatraeth oedd ffraeth eu llu.
Glasfedd eu hancwyn, a gwenwyn fu.

Y Gododdin (6th century)

(Men went to Catraeth, keen was their company.
They were fed on fresh mead, and it proved poison.)

Men went to Catraeth. The luxury liner
For three weeks feasted them.
They remembered easy ovations,
Our boys, splendid in courage.
For three weeks the albatross roads,
Passwords of dolphin and petrel,
Practised their obedience
Where the killer whales gathered,
Where the monotonous seas yelped.
Though they went to church with their standards
Raw death has them garnished.

Men went to Catraeth. The Malvinas
Of their destiny greeted them strangely.
Instead of affection there was coldness,
Splintering iron and the icy sea,
Mud and the wind's malevolent satire.
They stood nonplussed in the bomb's indictment.

Malcolm Wigley of Connah's Quay. Did his helm
Ride high in the war-line?
Did he drink enough mead for that journey?
The desolated shores of Tegeingl,
Did they pig this steel that destroyed him?
The Dee runs silent beside empty foundries.
The way of the wind and the rain is adamant.

Clifford Elley of Pontypridd. Doubtless he feasted.
He went to Catraeth with a bold heart.
He was used to valleys. The shadow held him.

The staff and the fasces of tribunes betrayed him.
With the oil of our virtue we have anointed
His head, in the presence of foes.

Phillip Sweet of Cwmbach. Was he shy before girls?
He exposed himself now to the hags, the glance
Of the loose-fleshed whores, the deaths
That congregate like gulls on garbage.
His sword flashed in the wastes of nightmare.

Russell Carlisle of Rhuthun. Men of the North
Mourn Rheged's son in the castellated vale.
His nodding charger neighed for the battle.
Uplifted hooves pawed at the lightning.
Now he lies down. Under the air he is dead.

Men went to Catraeth. Of the forty-three
Certainly Tony Jones of Carmarthen was brave.
What did it matter, steel in the heart?
Shrapnel is faithful now. His shroud is frost.
With the dawn the men went. Those forty-three,
Gentlemen all, from the streets and byways of Wales,
Dragons of Aberdare, Denbigh and Neath –
Figment of empire, whore's honour, held them.
Forty-three at Catraeth died for our dregs.

                                              Tony Conran

The Biggest Day

(*The Millennium Stadium in Cardiff opened with a prestigious sporting event in late September 1999, when Argentina played Wales at rugby. It was a truly breathtaking game. Simon Farrington wrote the following report for the 'Western Mail'.*)

On its biggest day, Wales got it right and stunned the world. The opening ceremony, powerful and emotional, played to our strengths – a land of song and heart.

The rugby wasn't great but victory was. And that was what

mattered on a day when Wales was in the spotlight and performed admirably.

Expectation was immense and with it came the nerves. And while more than 70,000 Welsh supporters released their adrenalin with rousing renditions of *Calon Lân* and the national anthem, the players – understandably – took more time to come down from the high that comes as part and parcel of a Rugby World Cup opening game.

It wasn't a perfect day; we didn't put 50 points on them, the electronic turnstiles went on strike and the Argentinians' kicker spent more time meditating then kicking, through he did that frustratingly well. And, as timings go, the Red Arrows missed the bus by minutes with their second fly-over midway through Argentina's national anthem.

But it was a day to be remembered. The sun did not shine, but our stars came out.

Children, the future of Wales and Welsh rugby, played an integral part of the opening ceremony and their performance was sensitively balanced with our nation's tradition.

The best male voice choirs launched into *Men of Harlech* and minutes later they had the biggest backup group in the world as *Bread of Heaven* bounced off the roof that was slowly easing back to reveal a grey sky.

The crowd was in great heart, buoyed by a few hours of lubricating vocal chords. The tension could be touched, and it flitted back and forth from the stands and over the pitch as great Welsh tries either side of half time failed to break the stubborn, hard-faced resistance of the Argentinians.

So Wales, as a team and nation, never truly relaxed. We revelled in the spotlight, delighted in the result and look forward to the next heart-stopping challenge. One step at a time.

Simon Farrington
The Western Mail, October 1st 1999

Culture

The Greatest Genius

I crossed over into the churchyard, ascended a green mound, and looked about me. I was now in the very midst of the Mynachlog Ystrad Fflur, the celebrated monastery of Strata Florida, to which in old times Popish pilgrims from all parts of the world repaired. The scene was solemn and impressive: on the north side of the river a large bulky hill looked down upon the ruins and the church, and on the south side, some way behind the farmhouse, was another which did the same. Rugged mountains formed the background of the valley to the east, down from which came murmuring the fleet but shallow Teifi. Such is the scenery which surrounds what remains of Strata Florida: those scanty broken ruins compose all which remains of that celebrated monastery, in which kings, saints and mitred abbots were buried, and in which, or in whose precincts, was buried Dafydd ap Gwilym, the greatest genius of the Cymbric race and one of the first poets of the world.

George Borrow (1803-1881)
Wild Wales

Beneath a Lovely Yew

(These lines are engraved on a memorial at the ruined abbey of Strata Florida, which was erected by the Honourable Society of Cymmrodorion in 1951.)

Dafydd, strong your muse's wine,
Is it here you were laid, beneath green boughs?
Beneath a lovely yew's blithe leaves
Song's been hidden where you're buried

Anon
Translated by Joseph P. Clancy

An Ineradicable Memory

For generations, most of my compatriots had crossed the border from Wales into England without realizing it. But I always realized it. For me, at quite an early age, it had become not a border but a frontier.

And we crossed it often. My father crossed it every Wednesday to the livestock market at Oswestry, as my grandfather had done before him. My father would not have called himself a Welsh Nationalist, but I remember sitting beside him as a boy in the trap behind the trotting pony when we passed a decrepit red brick column and he said, 'We're now crossing from Wales into England'. The memory is ineradicable, and must have been formative.

Our farm was less than two miles from that border. I had only to climb one of our high Berwyn Hills to look down at the English plain. We in our mountain valley spoke Welsh. They on the plain spoke English. We could sing spontaneously in harmony. They could not. We talked of preachers and of poets, they of footballers and racehorses. As a boy I was fascinated by the difference. As an adolescent I was disturbed by it.

Islwyn Ffowc Elis
in *Artists in Wales*
edited by Meic Stephens

What Passes and Endures

Still do the great mountains stay,
    And the winds above them roar;
There is heard at break of day
    Songs of shepherds as before.
Daisies as before yet grow
    Round the foot of hill and rock;
Over these old mountains, though,
    A new shepherd drives his flock.

To the customs of old Wales
  Changes come from year to year;
Every generation fails,
  One has gone, the next is here.
After a lifetime tempest-tossed
  Alun Mabon is no more
But the language is not lost
  And the old songs yet endure.

John Ceiriog Hughes (1832-1887)
Translated by Tony Conran

A Vineyard, Wales

EMRYS: Last night, Vortigern's couriers came with cruel
  tidings:
On the banks of the Dee two hosts today have descended,
From the east the Saxon, and the Pictish fleet from the north.
They wait till the swamps are dried by the winds of spring,
And at Easter they hasten towards Powys.
GARMON: What would'st thou of me?
EMRYS: God's nobleman, hearken,
A vineyard was set by man on a sunlit hill,
He hedged her, and planted within her the noblest vines,
He enclosed her strongly, and built a tower in her midst,
And to his son he gave her, a goodly heritage,
That his name might be known among men from age to age.
But a herd of swine have broken into the vineyard,
Have trampled the fence, and root and devour the vines;
Is it not well for the son to stand in the breach
And to call his friends to his aid,
That the breach may be closed and the heritage made secure?
Garmon, Garmon,
A vineyard placed in my care is Wales, my country,
To deliver unto my children
And my children's children
Intact, an eternal heritage:

And behold, the swine rush on her to rend her.
Now will I call on my friends,
Scholars and simple folk,
'Take your place by my side in the breach
That the age-old splendour be kept for ages to come.'
And this, my lord, is the vineyard of your Beloved too;
From Llan Fair to Llan Fair, a land where the Faith is
established.

Saunders Lewis (1893-1985)
from *Buchedd Garmon*
Translated by D.M. Lloyd

Relating to the Landscape

Like most people in rural Gwent, I had grown up largely ignorant of the meaning of the Welsh names for rivers, hills, farms, villages and towns that surrounded me, mispronouncing them in a way which has become habitual in the area. Understanding what the names meant released me into a new relationship with the landscape. The Viking explorers of the Atlantic isles and Greenland took care to name every prominent point along the coast where they landed; the naming in a sense reinvented the landscape, claimed it as human and habitable. In a similar way, learning Welsh, however inadequately, gave me a new and unexpected relation to the landscape, and made me realize how alienating it is to live out your life in ignorance of the meaning of names you use every day. Whether only subconsciously, many people in Gwent must feel this, and it may help explain the unease, the irrational hostility to Welsh that explodes there so readily . . .

John Barnie
in 'The Janus Country',
an essay included in *The King of Ashes* (1989)

On the Allotment

There they are,
the old man from the west,
the young girl from the south;
tending, as usual,
their adjacent allotments
on a cold spring morning.

Exchanging sprigs of vocabulary
between his half-forgotten mother tongue
and her half-learned second language,
as they nurture growth
from the hard soil of the valley.

The Welsh language binding them,
as light, as essential
as the clouds of their breath.

The shattered oak of a culture,
seeding in its old age;
the genes of a civilisation
defying death, determined to live.

Grahame Davies
Translated by the poet

The Man in Black

In the public library in the Town Hall of Rhyl, where the patient
books lie sheltered from the cacophonous uproar of Pleasureland
and the variegated mechanical marvels of the Marine Lake, I
discover to my amazed delight that Gerard Manley Hopkins lived
in Tremeirchion, just over the hill from our village, and learnt
Welsh. What else could a poet do? What a claim we had on the
world! What a birthright! This 'man in black', wrestling in secret
with our *cynghanedd*, was to have a revolutionary effect on the

137

making of poetry in an English language that was stretching itself to bestride the globe like a commercial Colossus. We had and we have our own manifest destiny. T.S. Eliot used to refer to the poetic process having the fortunate by-product of purifying the language of the tribe. Others have related the pollution of 'admass' to visible deterioration in the environment. We all have our responsibilities. In Wales this must involve the realisation that it is out of our language – our ancient language – that this landscape is best celebrated and renewed, the human environment cleansed, enriched, and renewed: the tidal wave of corrosive pollution stemmed. Take a year, take a lifetime, to hammer out a defence from this unique song that is *Cymraeg*.

Emyr Humphreys
from *Discovering Welshness* (1993)
edited by Oliver Davies and Fiona Bowie

Llety'r Eos

(*Llety'r Eos [the nightingale's lodging] is a house in the Hiraethog region. It was a traditional meeting place for local poets and singers. For a time Alun Llywelyn-Williams' sister lived there.*)

Surely the nightingale will not sing in this snowy night:
it is a mystery how the grey singer ever ventured,
some incredible summers ago, so far from the lowland
trees, so close to the pallid heavens of Hiraethog.

Eight hundred feet up, the snow begins to stick, the night
becomes bright; along the white hedges the car's wide
headlamps skate smoothly, but the wheels squeak 'careful!'
We slow down, and turn cautiously at the high crossroad.

We gape from our small guided world at the purity
of the calm sheepwalks' cosmos; the shut gates
slip past one by one, and the grey lines
of cowshed and cottage pour sleep to their centre.

Dark, chirpless, the sentinel grove on the brow of the hill;

but through the last welcoming gate, the lawn gleams,
a spotless glade, and the house beyond takes shape
from the white conquest like an enduring continent.

When the auto stands at the gate, when the door is opened,
the snow's smothering muteness is flung back to the night
by the voices of welcome, and the cheerful chat of the fire
and the light of fellowship on the hearth of the summerhouse of song.

Alun Llywelyn-Williams (1913-1988)
Translated by Joseph P. Clancy

The Birchtown Institute

There was a time when the Birchtown Institute was a very considerable place. The walls were distempered to match the prevailing shades of philosophic determinism. Acid overtones of radical dissent had eaten into the dark didactic murals. In the draughts room there was a plaque over the spot where Ramsay Macdonald had sat to play a game after being driven in by a cloudburst that had dispersed the open-air meeting he was holding in 1911. On the top of the main staircase was the photograph of a man who had shaken the hand of Gandhi.

At one time the lecture hall had boomed with orators, and thousands of members had developed a sort of eye-trouble known as 'magic lantern blink', brought on by too violently adjusting the eye-balls on hearing any sound similar to the rap of the pointer that introduced a change of slide. And Birchtown always seemed full of that type of sound. The smaller rooms of the Institute had been full of tight, intense classes of adult thinkers that had been going on for anything up to twenty years on topics ranging from the Seven Qualities of Godhead to the Fourteen Points of Wilson.

Now the lecture-room was silent and some climax of tedium and shabbiness had caused the last of the disputatious students to creep away from the smaller rooms. The rot had started with the anthropology class, the deepest-rooted comb in the whole thinking hive. One Thursday night they had suddenly stopped in mid-concept, feeling as old as the material they had been handling. And they had walked forth from the Institute renouncing all interest in man's beginnings. Their faces were blank, their eyes emptied of all the lighted curiosity of yesterday and their arms were anthropoidally adroop. Two of them had taken to Dadaism and the rest to drink.

Gwyn Thomas (1913-1981)
A Welsh Eye

In the National Museum

After seven years we returned,
like people in fairy-tales,
but a change had taken place.
We came back to a Wales
no longer wired to words –
its detonators sprung;
verbs, adjectives, defused –
mere phonemes, vaguely strung
in sticks of pseudo-talk:
its theme – the neatly-furled,
deadlocked, bedrocked concepts
of a fossil world.

On holiday as a boy
I hunted fossils out –
savoured the spiral core
silted with frozen grout,
locked in the matrix rock
like the lobe of a petrified brain;
treasured the whorl of quartz
spun from the still moraine,

and the golden feather of fern
pressed in the book of coal:
these are the fossils round which
living talk may roll.

Religion, politics: no.
They must beat with blood –
dart like protozoa
down the brain's warm flood;
brood upon the waters
within the curious eye
in the calm museum galleries
where the fossils lie –
then come down from those corridors,
history's upper reach,
to the strident two-way traffic
of meaningful speech.

Raymond Garlick

Song as Re-creation

I started singing in public in my father's chapel, Gibea, Brynaman
– in the Sunday School, the Band of Hope and the annual chapel
eisteddfod – all these institutions being, of course, thoroughly and
unselfconsciously Welsh in language. From there I graduated to
the village eisteddfod – where the winners from each chapel met
in combat, and the local Urdd eisteddfodau. Once I even managed
it to the stage of the Urdd National, singing penillion under
twelve. When my father moved to pastures new at Llanuwchllyn,
so far from the coal tips of the Aman valley. I found myself in
much the same round of chapel, Ysgol Sul, and eisteddfodau, and
my competitive career blossomed until my voice, as voices do,
broke.

By the time I found myself in college, I had a great yearning to
take part in the Welsh social functions (the Welsh social functions
being only a minor part of the general social functions of any

college in the University of Wales), and found myself often on stage. But I had nothing in particular I could do, so I eventually stumbled on a guitar, learnt a few chords and I've been writing songs and singing ever since.

My songs are of Wales and about Wales: love songs, satirical songs, funny songs and sad songs, religious songs and a few deliberately political songs. But all, or at least the better ones, reflect my feelings for my country, my people and my language, the Wales of today and my aspirations for the Wales of tomorrow.

When I write a song, I do so because a thought or an idea, an experience or an occasion, has struck a chord within me to which I want to give expression. I am always very conscious of the fact that I want to communicate. I always write with the audience in mind. Without an audience, there would be no song. (But having said that, and reflected on it, I also realise that I write songs for my own pleasure; and that to complete a song which pleases me is one of the most satisfying things in life.)

But essentially, I am in the communications business. And the great advantage I have over those who create in other fields is that I also have the opportunity to sing my own songs. To write a song is one thing, to communicate it successfully to an appreciative audience is to carry it a stage further, to give it greater depth and wider meaning, and every time it is so sung it is, in a sense, re-created.

Dafydd Iwan
in an essay in *Artists in Wales*
edited by Meic Stephens

A Language Learner

As he emerged from the swing doors of the hotel, the salty air lifted Roger's spirits and seemed to take the weight out of his limbs. He walked, he breathed, he admired the sunlight on the brave old towers of the castle, he looked with approval at the small boats riding the water of the harbour and the gulls riding the wind above them. Where a few words of Welsh reached him from a conversation in some shop doorway or sheltered corner, he slowed to listen, and it seemed to him that the shape and texture of the language were becoming familiar to him. In another few hours, that mysterious switch would turn itself on in his brain, and he would suddenly find that the intelligibility barrier was broken. Onward! The joy of learning a language, of exercising his professional aptitude, gave him a bracing sense of power and usefulness, matching the exhilaration that came from outside, from the sun and the strong air. His walk had refreshed him, he was ready to work again; not quite at full pressure, though. His eye fell on a newsagent's window. Yes! Get a Welsh newspaper, and sit quietly looking at it, getting some idea of mutations, puzzling out the vocabulary where possible, over a pint of beer. An excellent idea, typical of experienced and efficient Roger, scholarly, intellectual Roger, the brain-manager.

The shop yielded an unexpected treasure: the local paper, it seemed, put out a Welsh-language edition. Roger bore it away with a real sense of excited anticipation. He pushed open the door of the next pub he came to, careless of its quality, his eyes already picking out words on the front page.

John Wain (1925-1994)
A Winter in the Hills

The National

Let us visit the Crowning of the Bard at the National Eisteddfod, the annual celebration, or re-dedication, of Welshness at its most Welsh. For many Welsh people this is the supreme moment of the year, the perennial climax of the long resistance. The Eisteddfod is paripatetic in the Celtic tradition, being held in North and South Wales on alternate years. It is the largest folk festival in Europe, and its field really does look, from any nearby vantage point, rather like a military encampment – a huge assembly of tents, pavilions and caravans which in the course of the week becomes, like most fortifications in the front line, a bit muddy underfoot and a bit battered-looking around the sandbags. Its morale never flags though. Every day the immense crowds, drawn from all over Wales, wander and gossip around the wide central field, and music sounds incessantly over the loudspeakers, and visiting celebrities are snatched for television interviews, and there are poets striding here and there devising extempore verses for literary competitions, and male voice choirs spilling out of buses, and girls carrying harps, and stalls selling Welsh pop records, Dictionaries of Welsh Biography, manifestos for the Welsh Language Society or Daughters of the Dawn, patriotic car stickers, wooden figures of coracle men, T-shirts advertising the Welsh order of hope, scurrilous political broadsheets and many, many Bibles.

The unmistakable focus of it all is the great pavilion in the centre, said to be the largest portable building in the world, and there on the right day, if we can find ourselves in its cavernous interior, we will see the Welsh fire burning at its most theatrical. Assembled on stage are the Bards of the Druidical Order, a strange conclave of eminent citizens, doctors and philosophers, writers and politicians, dressed in long hooded robes of white and grey. They are presided over by ancient sages and attended by nymphs in green, by matrons with horns of plenty, by harpists and by trumpeters, and they are there to crown the winner of the chief poetry contest as Bard and hero of his nation – perhaps the greatest honour that the Cymry Cymraeg have to offer.

Jan Morris
Wales: The First Place (1998)

Druid

The druid, who could imagine him failing to be virile? It's unthinkable. His enormous shoulders, limitless eloquence, furious eyes, kind mouth, hair – long, white, wind-blown, dandruff free; and his toga, where did he get it? It's a profession that allows the best tea-tree shampoos and frequent foreign holidays. He wears plaited bands of pure gold, money torcs; sometimes, a broad collar across his breast and, when he's out, he carries a nifty sceptre. Invented after being slaughtered. A scholar whose ogam knowledge notched the stars, whose language named the weapons and the weeds of Gaul. Today, honoured in California and ridiculed in Cardiff. Ridiculed until a blue or green invitation to become one falls through the letterbox. And then how quickly slippery Iolo is easily forgiven. Caesar too explained. There are few as relaxed as an Archdruid and no-one better qualified to put a Crown on a poet's head, or place their hand on the shoulder of a poet who has won the Chair. When he does this, the Archdruid publicly praises the winning poet, at an intimate and at a ceremonial level, in a spectacle that is probably a unique television event. The exchange is spontaneous and completely public. The Archdruid both calms and elevates the need of his people to hear the hearth of their language burn.

David Greenslade
from his prose-poetry sequence
Cambrian Country (2000)

'A Language is Only Words'
(– Dafydd Elis Thomas)

The mountain is only a moorland,
The rock is only a stone.

I shan't see the skull in the crags of Tryfan
nor in the peat the bones of names
nor high rings on fairy pasture
or hoof-prints from Catraeth in the reeds.
I shan't see the 'moon above the valley'.
White eagles won't come here to nest.

I shan't hear its depths sound in spring water
nor the twisting wind on the nape of a thorn.
There aren't any legends rising from lakes
nor hopelessness out of the marsh.
Neither shall I hear the owl in Cowlyd.

I shan't think of pipe notes in the sedges;
I shan't remember the tune lamenting a Lark;
I'll not be reminded of tears by the name of a river.
Nor think of how giants have walked in this place,
raised walls, enclosed a homestead.

No, bogs don't sprout feathers.
There's no echo from the stone.
The mountain is only moorland.
Language is nothing but words.

Myrddin ap Dafydd
Translated by Tony Conran

The Spot

Why should I give a hang about Wales? It's by a mere fluke of fate
That I live in its patch. On a map it does not rate

Higher than a scrap of earth in a back corner,
And a bit of a bother to those who believe in order.

And who is it lives in this spot, tell me that.
Who but the dregs of society? Please, cut it out,

This endless clatter of oneness and country and race:
You can get plenty of these, without Wales, any place.

I've long since had it with listening to the croon
Of the Cymry, indeed, forever moaning their tune.

I'll take a trip, to be rid of their wordplay with tongue and with pen,
Back to where I once lived, aboard my fantasy's train.

And here I am then. Thank be for the loss,
Far from all the fanatics' talkative fuss.

Here's Snowdon and its crew; here's the land, bleak and bare;
Here's the lake and river and crag, and look, over there,

The house where I was born. But see, between the earth and the
heavens,
All through the place there are voices and apparitions.

I begin to totter somewhat, and I confess,
There comes over me, so it seems, a sort of faintness;

And I feel the claws of Wales tear at my heart.
God help me, I can't get away from this spot.

T.H. Parry-Williams (1887-1975)
Translated by Joseph P. Clancy

Combating Injustice

It is a strange experience for a middle-aged, non-political Englishman, whose life has been concerned with the celebration of non-violence, to see members of his family, his friends, his colleagues, his students, manhandled, arrested, taken through the courts, imprisoned: for non-violent protest against what appears to be official violation of the Welsh Language Act, civil rights, and equality before the law. I had not envisaged that a day would come when my wife, my sister-in-law, and seven other upright and peaceable citizens would be put on trial before a Crown Court. I had not foreseen that I should entertain, in my own study, two policemen come to take my son to Swansea gaol; that he would be imprisoned twice before his twentieth birthday. Contemplating photographs or eye-witness accounts of his being dragged by the hair in Carmarthen, beaten over the head in Llanrwst, stamped upon in the precincts of Manchester Magistrates' Court, kicked by several pairs of boots at Bangor, my reactions have been ambivalent. One reaction is a kind of relief that the return to health has been so total as to allow of such violent treatment, when so recently the slightest bruise was dangerous. The other reaction is righteous anger.

The history of Europe in the twentieth century has taught artists the need to harness their professional skills to combat injustice as soon as it manifests itself. When that injustice is concerned with language, the responsibility of the writer – whatever his language – is the greater. For those who write in English as one of the languages of Wales, it is unthinkable that it should be debased to the level of a crude political dialect, to oppress and defraud Welsh of the equal validity with which natural justice and, apparently, law endow it.

Raymond Garlick
from an essay included in *Artists in Wales*
edited by Meic Stephens

Offa's Dyke 1 (Customs Office) 2000 AD?

You ask me to define myself;
You offer me official words to use.
Cap in hand I stand,
Confused but not amused.

'Welsh,' you state. 'That is your style.
Write it there on the form –
A Welsh Welshman. Make it clear.'

'Won't English do?' I ask. 'Or British?'

You are incredulous and suspicious, too,
Of yet another wriggle of my perfidy.
How can I show what I think I know
To be the truth for me?

You point with ease at all the evidence:
Pontlottyn birth, dark hair, broad face
And Biblical Welsh name. To you even the twist
And lilt of my replies are Welsh enough.

'Mother-tongue,' I say, 'That's how I know.
'Tis English.' Then, up you flare:
'What do the English care?'

Strangely to you, and not quite clear to me,
My answer comes: 'Tis I who care, not they.'
And so we face our double-sided truth:
You'll not give up; neither can I.
'I can't go forward, then?' 'No.
You must remain here, on the frontier,
Nationality confused; yourself by tongue not birth abused.'

Reluctantly I turn and go . . .
No choice remains for me –
Only a measured inching forward,
A hope to find identity in what I do, and love, and know.

R. George Thomas

Religion

The Other

There are nights that are so still
that I can hear the small owl calling
far off and a fox barking
miles away. It is then that I lie
in the lean hours awake listening
to the swell born somewhere in the Atlantic
rising and falling, rising and falling
wave on wave on the long shore
by the village, that is without light
and companionless. And the thought comes
of that other being who is awake, too,
letting our prayers break on him,
not like this for a few hours,
but for days, years, for eternity.

R.S. Thomas (1913-2000)

Evening Service

We had come to evening service through the shower,
By the set time, a precious few of us,
Taking our seats in the chapel here and there,
Not a full pew to be seen in the whole place.
And I observed, attendance was so poor,
And the ones there soaked almost to the skin,
That one old dear would raise a pale blue sprig
Next to her nostrils every now and then.
The preacher, as the clock was nearing seven,
Fully endorsed the Psalmist's ancient cry,
Uttered amid the depths of grief so often,
Proclaiming God a refuge and a strength;
And the scent of 'old-man' to this old woman was
A very present help in her distress.

T.H. Parry-Williams (1887-1975)
Translated by Joseph P. Clancy

St. David's Day

By a rope across his nape, beneath his armpits,
The saint dragged a plough of wood, and broke the ground.
Then barefoot he would tramp the clods, the cant
Of the furrow beneath his sole a long delight.
God's zealous ox, his strength; his holy lust –
Husbandman of a nation's seasons on his strip.
He worked a stony tilth beneath the rock,
Made the slopes fertile and uprooted the thorns.
He sowed the seed that after death became
Christ's bread for thousands at the boards of grace.
Christ's scripture ornament was his rough headland,
A hard securing of the saints' beginnings.
If only after our swift ploughs we sowed
Today the grains his right hand smoothly spread.

Arms dump and aerodrome have shared the saint's headland
And up above purrs a contented hell,
Its docile dancers underneath hard at it
Serving the voracious rows of teeth of steel.
Eternal tents of Mammon – here they take
My poor bemuddled folk into their plot,
The plaited paint entangling them like eels
And the easy craze of many in one spot.
Power of David, should it cross the heather as a tempest
The tents of Mammon would not be left standing on the field;
It would whirl their whole providence of puff and sham
And the proper claims of blood to streaming ribbons,
And the long insolence and pollution of the pound
Would dance the dried leaves' dance in the high wind.

Waldo Williams (1904-1971)
Translated by Joseph P. Clancy

The Shrine

The shrine of St. David is on the north side of the chancel; the single stone which composed it is now broken into many pieces. In the side are four recesses, into which the notaries dropped their offerings, and the monks removed them through doors behind. Our kings frequently made pilgrimages to this shrine, where they paid their devotions to the saint, then in the highest repute. In the year 1080 William the Conqueror invaded Wales with a large army, proceeding in a hostile manner till he came as far as St. David's; but there he laid aside the warrior for the votary, and reconciled the princes of the land to the homage he exacted, by the splendour of his offerings, and the humility of his deportment.

Benjamin Heath Malkin (1769-1842)
The Scenery, Antiquities and Biography of South Wales

Ancient Monument : St. Non's at St. David's

(after reading the Department of Environment pamphlet)

No clue to its date or function in the ruins:
no distinctive features survive.

Not orientated in Christian west-east,
not probably the remains of an earlier building.

No skeletons in the stone coffins,
not even the Blessed Non.

No certain connection with the early Christian pillar:
no one knows why this pillar-stone is propped here.

Not used for religion after the Reformation – first
non-chapel, then converted house, then leek-garden.

No pilgrimages now to the well
no longer used for curing non-sight.

No exact location of St. David's birthplace in the *Life* –
no proof of the story of his birth on this spot: how

Non, his mother, did not save herself from rape;
no sign of the stone imprinted by Non's fingers in birthpains –

Non, perhaps not a woman at all, but the male saint Nonna.
No fee to visit St. Non's.

Gladys Mary Coles

Ffynnon Fair

(Joan Abbott Parry was drowned in the sea at Ffynnon Fair, Llŷn, in July 1904, shortly before her sixteenth birthday. Her younger brother saw her fall, and broke the news first to their father: 'Father, I must whisper this . . . ')

The men saw the sway of blue serge dress caught
On rocks by Ffynnon Fair, and lifted her above the swell,
Climbed the rough steps with the tide's burden between
Them, the unutterable. How she must have, as she fell,
Caught her breath, clutched at startled air, before blue-green
Surge of sea clutched and kept her gasp.

Her father drew a line and shadow on sunlit page,
Defined the shape of Ynys Enlli, their pilgrimage.
Father, I must whisper this, her brother said
My sister has fallen.

Now the women of the parish lay her out
And wash her. Their hands only are able to define
Her high cheek-bone, young breast, they know like lovers
The thin-ridged beauty of her spine.
They tease the flecks of seaweed from her hair.

I must whisper this.

Each year her mother turned the legend of the well:
*A woman's unutterable wish fulfilled by water
Carried from the perfect shape of Ffynnon Fair
Unspilt, up to the clifftop church.* Her daughter
In this, her fifteenth year, took down a cup.

Father, I must whisper this.

Perhaps she broke the water's surface first, and spoke her wish.
The women of the parish know her prayer.
Her mother understood her faith.
With the salt taste caught in her own breath,
She whispers all of it to be undone,
To see her daughter climb the broken steps again,
Holding whole her own life, like unspilt water.

Michael Ponsford

St. Winefride's Well
(After Winefride's raising from the dead and the breaking out of the fountain.)

Oh now while skies are blue, now while seas are salt
    While rushy rains shall fall or brooks shall fleet from fountains,
While sick men shall cast sighs, of sweet health all despairing,
    While blind men's eyes shall thirst after daylight, draughts of
        daylight
Or deaf ears shall desire that lipmusic that's lost upon them,
While cripples are, while lepers, dancers in dismal limb dance,
    Fallers in dreadful frothpits, waterfearers wild,
Stone, palsy, cancer, cough, lung-wasting, womb not bearing
    Rupture, running sores, what more? In brief, in burden,
As long as men are mortal and God merciful,
    So long to this sweet spot, this leafy lean-over,
This dry dene, now no longer dry nor dumb, but moist and
        musical
With the uproll and the downcarol of day and night delivering
Water, which keeps thy name, (for not in rock written,
But in pale water, frail water, wild rash and reeling water,
That will not wear a print, that will not stain a pen,
Thy venerable record, virgin, is recorded)
Here to this holy well shall pilgrimages be,
And not from purple Wales only nor from elmy England,
But from beyond seas, Erin, France and Flanders every where,
Pilgrims, still pilgrims, more pilgrims, still more poor pilgrims.
What sights shall be when some that swung, wretches, on crutches

Their crutches shall cast from them, on heels of air departing,
Or they go rich as roseleaves hence that loathsome came hither!
Not now to name even
Those dearer, more divine boons whose haven the heart is.

    As sure as what is most sure, sure as that spring
primroses shall new-dapple next year, sure as to-morrow
morning, amongst come-back-again things, things with
a revival, things with a recovery.
Thy name [*Winefride will live*] . . .

Gerard Manley Hopkins (1844-1889)

Glass
In Llanrhaeadr yng Nghinmeirch

(*The church of St. Dyfnog in the Denbighshire village of Llanrhaeadr yng Nghinmeirch is renowned for its very fine Jesse window.*

During the Civil War the window was removed, hidden in a large chest and buried in nearby woodland in order to protect it from the Parliamentarians.)

The pedigree of Christ, though scattered once,
A rare but broken picture in a chest
Interred, its precious colours rose again
To brilliantly proclaim God's hope to earth.
And here, I like to think, there stood a bard
To read the poetry of the lead and glass
Before he sang his covenantal hymn
To grace which neither world nor grace erodes.

Through this same Jesse window did I gaze
One summer's day, unburdened by a care,
Upon that miracle of filtered blue,
But seeing the smirking crack which breached the wall
I know I too would never willingly
Believe that journey's end should be a chest.
Is it the image or the hope which gives
Me hope? I have a pane no grave can hold.

Enid Wyn Baines
Translated by Gwynn Matthews

An Elegant Place

Friday, 19, 1779. I preached near the market-place, and afterwards rode over to Trefeca. Howell Harris' house is one of the most elegant places which I have ever seen in Wales. The little chapel and all things round about it are finished in an uncommon taste, and the gardens, orchards, fish-ponds and mount adjoining make the place a little paradise. He thanks God for these things and looks through them. About six-score persons are now in the

Family – all diligent, all constantly employed, all fearing God and working righteousness. I preached at ten to a crowded audience, and in the evening at Brecon again, but to the poor only, the rich (a very few excepted) were otherwise employed.

John Wesley (1703-1791) in his Journal

John Elias Advises His Son

(In a letter addressed to his son the Calvinistic Methodist minister John Elias (1774-1871) writes with the daunting force of his conviction. The letter, of which this is only part, was written at Llanfechell in 1819.)

Satan has some design in filling thy heart with distracting thoughts of that kind. Perhaps his aim is this, to decoy thee to his service!

. . . O the depth of Satan's devices, and his awful blasphemies! O that thou mightest come to know those destructive devices and temptations, and also to withstand him firmly in the faith, and oppose him in the following manner, saying, 'Satan, I have heard of thy crafty devices and snares; now I experience and begin to know them. Thou chief enemy of God, and destroyer of men; how, by the pride, didst rebel against God, and by that didst lose a blissful habitation thy Maker place thee in, and through envy at our first parents in their happy state, didst succeed in bringing them into a miserable condition, by tempting them to sin against God.

John Elias
The Life and Letters of John Elias
edited by Edward Morgan (1973)

Civil and Respectful

I have got a yearning for the Welsh people and could find it in my heart to work for their conversion. However on consideration it seems best to turn my thoughts elsewhere. I say this because, though I am not my own master, yet if people among us shew a zeal and aptitude for a particular work, say foreign missions, they can commonly get employed on them. The Welsh are very civil and respectful but do not much come to us and those who are converted are for the most part not very staunch. They are much swayed by ridicule. Wesleyanism is the popular religion. They are said to have a turn for religion, especially what excites outward fervour, and more refinement and pious feeling than the English peasantry but less steadfastness and sincerity.

Gerard Manley Hopkins (1844-1889)
in a letter (1874)

Llanrhaeadr-ym-Mochnant

This is where he sought God.
And found him? The centuries
Have been content to follow
Down passages of serene prose.

There is no portrait of him
But in the gallery of
The imagination: a brow
With the hair's feathers
Spilled on it; a cheek
Too hollow; rows of teeth
Broken on the unmanageable bone
Of language; in this small room
By the river expiating the sin
Of his namesake.
              The smooth words
Over which his mind flowed
Have become an heirloom. Beauty
Is how you say it, and the truth,
Like this mountain-born torrent,
Is content to hurry
Not too furiously by.

R.S. Thomas (1913-2000)

At Bala

It seethed beneath wind and rain
Last night, Ceridwen's cauldron;
Now, irresistible grace,
Llyn Tegid's been converted.
It has disappeared, assumed
Into the clear calm morning.

We could walk uphill across
Looking-glass land on branches
To the top, and hop a cloud
From Bala to Llanuwchllyn.
Instead, we stroll hand in hand,
Heading for nowhere special;
Sedate middle-aged lovers,
Spring harvest, we take our time.
We let the lakeside lead us
By green pastures where March lambs
Wobble to milk tranquil ewes.
Over a rise, past posted
Information on fishing,
Through a screen of yew our eyes
Are drawn to a small stone church,
A plot planted with headstones.

This might be any village
Churchyard whose stones speak Welsh
Posed for a picture postcard.
But the not uncommon names,
Thomas Charles, Lewis Edwards,
Pierce the placid morning's glass.
They kindle fire in the thatch
Of memory. At Bala
Christ was raised in sinfast hearts;
God's barefoot Word crossed mountain
And ocean with prints of flame
Struck glowing from this brazier.
The Arans and Arenigs
Rejoiced to leap in its light.

The great limbs shift in their sleep
Under cloudshade and sunlight.
We turn to walk the lakeside,
More scenery, now, than shrine,
Back to the town, clouds hover,

As hushed as a burnt-out heart.
A bush stirs. The breeze begins
To move upon the waters.

Joseph Clancy

The Man in the Box

(*In his novel 'Rhys Lewis', Daniel Owen draws on personal recollection in his description of childhood chapel-going.*)

It was open, rows of backless benches running across it, and a few deep seats being ranged around the walls. In the centre there was a large stove, surrounded always by a crowd of children with faces red as a cock's comb. Most likely the season was winter.

I remember the Big Seat, the Singers' Seat to its left, and Abel Hughes, with his velvet cap, stationed under the pulpit, going about every now and then to snuff the candles. The pulpit was built against the wall, so high up that it reminded me of the swallow's nest left under the eaves of our house during the previous summer. It puzzled me how 'the man' (so I styled him) who was in the pulpit could have climbed thither, and what was his object in doing so? Was it a habit of his, and did he ever get a fall in descending, as I did more than once in coming downstairs? Did someone carry him down, as my brother Bob used to carry me?

I wondered greatly no one had a word to say but 'the man in the box', and still more that he should have so much. I understood not a word of it all with the exception of 'Jesus Christ', and I fancied at first *he* was the 'Jesus Christ' whom my mother so often spoke to me about. I was expecting him every moment to stop talking; but in vain. After he had spoken a long time, according to my reckoning, he put on a fierce look, flushed in the face, and shouted loudly. I made up my mind then that he was not Jesus Christ. I fancied him to be 'giving it' me rather badly – what for I did not know; but he looked at me so often that I knew well enough it was to me he was referring. So thinking, I began to cry again, and had to be half suffocated a second time, and given another Nelson ball before I ceased my noise.

I looked about me, upstairs and down, and wondered at seeing so many people in the gallery. Were they in the habit of sleeping there? How did they get beds enough? I found the chapel darkening, and the man in the box looking smaller, and appearing to retreat farther and farther away from me, although he kept on shouting, higher and still higher. I felt myself gathered to my mother, and suddenly – in profoundest slumber – lost sight of everybody and everything. I don't know how long I slept; but they had great trouble in waking me, despite the singing of the congregation.

Daniel Owen (1836-1895)
Rhys Lewis
Translated by James Harris

Sabbath Breaking

'Is that gentlewoman your wife?'
  'She is no gentlewoman, sir, but she is my wife.'
  'Of what religion are you?'
  'We are Calvinistic-Methodists, sir,'
  'Have you been to chapel?'
  'We are just returned, sir.'

Here the woman said something to her husband, which I did not hear, but the purport of which I guessed from the following question which he immediately put.

  'Have you been to chapel, sir?'
  'I do not go to chapel; I belong to the Church.'
  'Have you been to church, sir?'
  'I have not – I said my prayers at home, and then walked out.'
  'It is not right to walk on the Sabbath day, except to go to church or chapel.'
  'Who told you so?'
  'The law of God, which says you shall keep holy the Sabbath day.'
  'I am not keeping it unholy.'

'You are walking about, and in Wales when we see a person walking idly about, on the Sabbath day, we are in the habit of saying "Sabbath breaker, where are you going?"'

'The Son of Man walked through the fields on the Sabbath day, why should I not walk along the roads?'

'He who called Himself the Son of Man was God, and could do what He pleased, but you are not God.'

'But He came in the shape of a man to set an example. Had there been anything wrong in walking about on the Sabbath day, He would not have done it.'

Here the wife exclaimed, 'How worldly-wise these English are!'

'You do not like the English,' said I.

'We do not dislike them,' said the woman; 'at the present they do us no harm, whatever they did of old.'

'But you still consider them,' said I, 'the seed of Y Sarfes cadwynog, the coiling serpent.'

'I should be loth to call any people the seed of the serpent,' said the woman.

'But one of your great bards did,' said I.

'He must have belonged to the Church, and not to the chapel then,' said the woman. 'No person who went to chapel would have used such bad words.'

George Borrow (1801-1881)
Wild Wales

Drink and Religion

The first request that William Havard the preacher would make on reaching his lodgings, after preaching a powerful sermon, would be for a quart of beer, and no-one doubted his piety. But imagine what would happen today if the Reverend Morgannwg Jones were to make the same request? The news would spread throughout Wales and he would be in disgrace and damned for ever. The Reverend Morgannwg Jones has as great a thirst as old William Havard, but public opinion has changed after fifty years of enlightenment. It is possible, my friend, if you and I are spared for another fifty years that we shall regard those things which today are essential for our welfare as evils to be avoided like poison.

> Daniel Owen (1836-1895)
> *Gwen Tomos*
> Translated by T. Ceiriog Williams and E.R. Harries

Glamorgan and Carmarthenshire

Tomos Lewis[1] of Talyllychau,
His hammersound in the forge like bells
Over the village, abbey and the swans on the lake;
He drew his hymn like a horseshoe from the fire,
Struck it on the anvil of the Holy Ghost
And in it set the nails of Calvary Hill.

And Williams of Pantycelyn[2] himself
Would be at my elbow in Llansadwrn
Tutoring my voice in the pattern of his song;
But I lost the yearning to look on his face
In the town square up there on my soapbox,
His fine voice drowned by the drum of the crane.

It was not for any industrial worker
To wander through the plant and mills like a pilgrim

With empty pockets and a pack on his back:
    On Saturday nights we rose for the justice
    Of our cause, and on Sunday sang your hymns:
Mabon[3] and *Caeo*[4]; Keir Hardie[5] and *Crug-y-bar*.

    The span of the Cross is greater by far
    Than their Puritanism and their Socialism,
And the fist of Karl Marx has a place in His Church:
    Farm and furnace are one together in His estate,
    The humanity of the pit, the piety of the country:
Tawe and Tywi, Canaan and Wales, earth and heaven.

D. Gwenallt Jones (1899-1968)
Translated by Ned Thomas and B.S. Johnson

Translators' notes:
[1] Tomos Lewis (1759-1842), hymn-writer and blacksmith.
[2] Williams of Pantycelyn, William Williams (1717-91), hymn-writer.
[3] Mabon, William Abraham (1842-1922), miners' leader.
[4] *Caeo . . . Crug-y-bar*, hymn-tunes.
[5] Keir Hardie (1856-1915), miners' leader and founder of the Independent Labour Party, Member of Parliament for Merthyr Tydfil.

A Preaching Debut

After three weeks of anxious suspense came that Sunday night when he was to preach for the first time. As he sat, shy and nervous in the pulpit before the service began, he watched the people streaming into their pews, some of them belonging to other sects and some who were members of no denomination at all. It was, he reflected, quite a formidable enough undertaking to face the Siloam congregation itself, without being made to feel like a preacher at 'big meetings' for the first time.

He looked through his hymnbook for the hymns he had chosen, carefully marking the pages with slips of paper. Looking up, he hurriedly bent his head to hide a smile. In one of the rear pews sat George Hobley, Huw Jones and other men from his quarry-gallery, while on the other side of the chapel, near the door, was

Robin Evans. *Yr argian*, who would slip in next? His grandfather Dafydd Ellis? No, that drunken old reprobate could not set foot outside his house now – a matter for thanksgiving, perhaps.

During the earlier part of the service Owen felt acutely nervous and selfconscious and occasionally, particularly when he happened to look at George Hobley trying to appear quite as much at home as if he were at the bar of the Crown, he badly wanted to laugh. But as he glanced round the chapel again during the announcements and collection his shyness changed to a feeling of deep, quiet happiness. Instinctively but surely he knew that the kindhearted, sincere people in front of him were wishing him well, were watching him confidently and trustfully, eager to be able to rejoice in his success. Whatever the future might bring he *had* to prove himself worthy of them and their trust in him, of the homely society and neighbourhood in which he had been brought up.

T. Rowland Hughes (1903-1949)
The Beginning
Translated by Richard Ruck

The Coming of Evan Roberts

On reaching the village he found the roadway thronged, as it had been the night before, with hundreds of eager men and women who had thought it no trouble to walk many miles from their homes on the chance of being able to hear Evan Roberts, or at least to catch a glimpse of him.

The chapel was full to overflowing, the courtyard too, and the surrounding slope. It was impossible any one could hear the evangelist, except those who were inside the chapel; but they could join in the singing, and perhaps the Spirit would visit them in the open air! So they adjourned to the flat on which the kiln stood, and there in the twilight they held their prayer meeting, with only the pale blue sky of evening over them.

When the singing from the chapel swept out on the breeze they joined their voices to the swelling strains, and the evangelist, standing in the pulpit, caught the sound through the open doorway, and was cheered and uplifted into a fervour of spiritual warmth which spread to the crowd around him. His clear earnest eyes scanned the throng of eager faces; he saw the rough hands clasped in nervous tension, and with the spiritual intuition of a 'Sensitive', he seemed to feel the unrest of their souls, to hear the cry of their most secret longings; and moved to the heart by their expectant faces, he set himself to answer their call.

Allen Raine (1836-1908)
Queen of the Rushes

The Voice of a Prophet

(As a young man in 1905 P.G. Wodehouse was commissioned by a newspaper to cover the evangelical revival in Wales. He found Evan Roberts a truly charismatic figure and when, years later, he wrote his novel 'Ukeridge' he fictionalised Roberts, giving him the name Evan Jones.)

This was the first time I had had occasion to attend one of these revival meetings, and the affect it had on me was to make me feel as if I had been imbibing large quantities of champagne to the accompaniment of a very loud orchestra. Even before the revivalist rose to speak, the proceedings had had an effervescent quality singularly unsettling to the sober mind, for the vast gathering had begun to sing hymns directly they took their seats; and while the opinion I have formed of the inhabitants of Llanindnno was not high, there was no denying their vocal powers. There is something about a Welsh voice when raised in song that no other voice seems to possess – a creepy, heart-searching quality that gets right into a man's inner consciousness and stirs it up with a pole. And on top of this had come Evan Jones's address.

It did not take me long to understand why this man had gone through the countryside like a flame. He had magnetism, intense earnestness and the voice of a prophet crying in the wilderness. His fiery eyes seemed to single out each individual in the hall, and every time he paused sighings and wailings went up like smoke in a furnace. And then, after speaking for what I discovered with amazement on consulting my watch was considerably over an hour, he stopped. And I blinked like an aroused somnambulist, shook myself to make sure I was still there, and came away.

P.G. Wodehouse (1881-1985)
Ukeridge

Sermons

ESTER. Blissful, father bach, was the sermon of Spurgeon Evans at the preaching match. My kerchief is still wet with my tears.

JOSI (*cold and impartially*). Tidy enough. Quite cute, too, was the sermon of Ben Watkin.

ESTER. Your sense is odder than your face! Must I feel ashamed that I am your daughter? And you one of the four deacons – one of the four Big Heads in Capel Sion. Ben's sermon was like a tub of butter with the last churning on the top. It is middling in the middle and rancid at the bottom where the dealer can't smell. Spurgeon is a champion preacher when eloquence waggles his tongue.

JOSI. Sermons preached with a view to a capel are like buying a cow in calf; you do not know what she will bring forth – if she brings forth at all. And they are spotted with too much babbling praise.

ESTER. But Spurgeon prayed for the Big Heads.

JOSI (*earnestly*) The Big Heads are past praying for. You cannot pray for saints. He was a job to do that. Why did he not pray for the congregation? But he is only a stripling of a student from College Carmarthen.

ESTER. He preached the sweetest sermon I ever heard. Which of the two will you Big Heads choose to minister in Sion – Ben Watkin or Spurgeon?

JOSI. You are a prattling wench.

ESTER. Ho! And you will vote for Ben Watkin! You are a sorry sermon taster.

JOSI. Where is the light in your dense talk?

Caradoc Evans (1878-1945)
Taffy

Beware of the Cinema

Beware of the cinema, boys of the town,
Her black secret, folds are the enemies gown,
She schools souls in evil, she wipes out all worth
She ravages innocence, beauty, at birth.
A wolfe by the wayside, a black bird of prey,
The cinema strikes at the end of the day.
Peering at a poster a menace is near,
The devil himself lying low in the rear.
Bewitched and bewildered through black gates they go
Slinging their gold in the jaws of the foe.
The heavens are weeping, the angels they sigh,
Fools where's your fear? The end is now nigh,
Lusts and corruption did it for Rome
Now the same evil stalks us at home.
Wales watch your treasures, they are trampled in mud,
Your sabbath and chapel is worth more than your blood.

The Reverend Thomas David Evans
circa 1930

Inviting the Wrath of God

To my shame, I didn't make even a routine objection when, the following Sunday evening, Sinclair took me to the cinema. I was still a child when the plebiscite was held on Sunday cinemas. The family had turned up *en masse* to vote against a measure which seemed to invite the immediate wrath of God on our town. The Rev. Thomas Ll. Fabian had preached the previous evening on the Book of the Prophet Isaiah, the first chapter and the ninth verse, 'Except the LORD of hosts had left unto us a very small remnant, we should have been as Sodom, and we should have been like unto Gomorrah'. My father had, for some reason, not been in chapel that night, and in the face of bewildered and sorrowful family opposition (Grandpa Vivyan was, of course, still alive), he

placidly maintained that if people wanted to go to the pictures on
Sunday, let them get on with it. Nevertheless, despite my father's
laissez-faire shrug of the shoulders (which did not become him),
neither of my parents would have gone within a mile of a cinema
on a Sunday. But I was getting used to breaking strict family
taboos. It was worth breaking any number of taboos to see the
Beatles (we had had to wait some time for the film to reach Wales)
in blissfully ideal circumstances – in the back row of the Ritz with
Sinclair's arm around my shoulders and his other hand puddling
mine.

Moira Dearnley
That Watery Glass (1973)

Tabernacle

Great was Windsor-Daniel, but greater – so they told – was Eben
L. Pembroke. Once a year in the month of November Tabernacle
sets apart a Sunday for a preaching feast, when the pulpit is
occupied by the sweetest preacher that money can bring to it.
Welsh is the speech of the Sunday morning sermon but English is
the evening's, because at the evening sermon feast sit many
honourable Welsh who have forgotten their language. On such a
Sunday the preacher was Eben L. Pembroke, who had fame in
America for his lovely sermons and was called 'God's
Lovemonger', and all his sermons were on the text 'God is Love'.
Tabernacle could not contain all the people who came to its door,
but for the more honourable room was made in the Big Seat, chairs
having been borrowed from the Crown and Anchor. Amos, his
Box-Bible on the ledge before him, vowed that soon he would be
as genteel as the most honourable. Perhaps next year or the year
after he would be among them, enjoying the obscene photographs
of Duke-Dan Grocer, the lewd matchbox of Sir Devon-Davies, the
imitation cigarettes of Sam Lawyer, the fountain pen of Williams

Contractor, and the ornamented marbles of Goliath Jones Parliament.

Caradoc Evans (1878-1945)
Nothing to Pay

Capel Mawr

It all started with a little booklet called *Rhodd Mam* (Mother's Gift) that never came as a gift from any mother anyway, but rather as a treasure donated to your Sunday School teacher. It was basically an elementary catechism, ruthless in doctrine, and the hinge question to me was 'How many kinds of children are there?' The answer; sharp as a rapier thrust, was: 'Two kinds. Good children and bad children'.

Because you had been netted into *Capel Mawr* from the beginning of all time and almost rivetted three times a Sunday to seat 22, not to mention the midweek meeting, carving names and designs on the back of Seat 23, you developed a saintly determination to be good, a determination that has remained with me. Religion in those days, Nonconformity at least, had been reduced to its lowest possible common denominator: Christianity meant trying to love your neighbour, never doing anybody any deliberate harm, trying to act as much as you could according to the dictates of the ten commandments and the pulpit god, learning verses for Sunday morning, mastering tonic-sol-fa for the hymn's sake and honouring your parents, not that there was anything in particular you could do about avoiding the latter in those sterner days.

The hard-line days of expelling big-bellied girls and having to believe that a whale swallowed Jonah or that Jonah swallowed a whale had gone. God was largely the Old Testament God who would make it thunder if you whistled on Sunday (not that anybody would particularly want to whistle in Llanrwst on

Sunday) or who would frown openly from the skies if you went to bathe naked in the Big River on a hot summer day.

T. Glynne Davies (1926-1976)
from an essay included in *Artists in Wales*
edited by Meic Stephens

Lost Faith

There were no rabbits on the quarry bank. The last gunshot had sent them into hiding. But it was a warm place, sheltered from the wind and Griff threw himself on the ground to rest. J.T. followed more carefully, sitting down on an outcrop of stone. The quarry itself was small and overgrown with brambles.

– We should have brought a dog, Griff said, rolling over on his belly to be able to look up to where J.T. was sitting.

– Sent him in there. That quarry is teeming with game.

J.T. nodded and searched his pockets for a handkerchief to wipe the sweat off his face.

– You look like a crowned bard, sitting up there, Griff said.

– I'm afraid there's no poetry in me, J.T. said. I wish there was. The truth is I can no more write a verse than shoot a pheasant. I feel the loss, I do really.

– Far too many poets in Wales, anyway, Griff said. Look at our col. Regular tommy-rot factory.

J.T. smiled and scratched his head.

– In every respect, Griff said.

He fell silent, pulling at a long stem of grass as if he could say more and preferred not to.

– What do you mean?

J.T. leaned towards him to catch what he might murmur.

– I don't believe any of it, Griff said.

He kept his gaze fixed steadily on J.T.'s face gauging the effect of his words.

– Not one word, he said.

J.T. said nothing. The hum of the wild bees in the brambles on the edge of the quarry nearest to where they sat seemed to grow louder in the silence. At last J.T. cleared his throat.

– Do you mean, he said hoarsely, do you mean you've lost your faith?

– If that's the way you want to put it, Griff said. I just can't go on swallowing it all any more.

– Swallowing what? J.T. said.

– Talking about God as if he were the Moderator of the Free Church Council, Griff said. As though our denomination owned him and kept him in a box under the pulpit and stood on it every Sunday. As if he went over the accounts of every chapel with the two other members of the Trinity and signed them with 'examined and found correct'.

Griff made a gesture with the stem of grass as if it were a pen and he was signing a document with a flourish.

– I admit there is too much emphasis on organization in our Connexion, J.T. said slowly. There is too much talk about collections and funds and . . .

– Listen, Griff said. I'm not arguing. I'm confessing. I don't believe a single word of any of it.

J.T. lifted his gun with his hand as if he were about to say something.

– Is that gun loaded? Griff said.

J.T. slipped the catch and opened the gun.

– No, he said, looking up at Griff, who laughed.

– Thought you wanted to shoot me, Griff said.

Emyr Humphreys
Outside the House of Baal (1965).

Surfing

Surfing the radio, looking for a blast
of Satch or Stan or Dizzy, I hit on
an allelujah programme telling me
that all I had to do was love the Lord,
let Jesus in my life and all that jazz,
backed up by loud amens and in a voice
like Billy Graham dipped in soul. Shortwave, of course.

I stuck it for a while, then switched it off,
and thought how simple it would be if I,
a Church in Wales agnostic, could be sure
I'd find salvation in this other way,
shouting the praises of a zapped-up Lord,
letting a swinging Jesus into my heart,
pumping my neighbour's hand in ecstasy,
kissing his wife's plump cheek in Christian love.

And then I thought of men who, dungeon-deep
(and women too, we must be clear in this),
sing out their praises in a private way,
touching the Lord with humble, furtive hands,
scarce knowing who he is, or where, or why,
and of the desolation in the souls
of those who, hoping still that he exists,
can never quite be sure, and die their deaths
without the certain hope of this and that.

And so we must continue with this life,
each in his strange pursuit of what is good,
frail to the last, nailed to our cross of hope,
some with loud voices, others in silent prayer,
hitting on something, moving on to the next,
filling out time till time fills us with dust.

Herbert Williams